Holy Silence

Holy Silence

Michael Hickey

HAMILTON BOOKS
AN IMPRINT OF
ROWMAN & LITTLEFIELD
Lanham • Boulder • New York • London

Published by Hamilton Books
An imprint of The Rowman & Littlefield Publishing Group, Inc.
4501 Forbes Boulevard, Suite 200, Lanham, Maryland 20706
www.rowman.com

86-90 Paul Street, London EC2A 4NE, United Kingdom
British Library Cataloguing in Publication Information Available

Library of Congress Cataloging-in-Publication Data

Names: Hickey, Michael, 1973– author.
Title: Holy silence / Mike Hickey.
Description: Lanham, MD : Hamilton Books, an imprint of Rowman & Littlefield
    [2022] | Includes bibliographical references and index. | Summary: "Looking at
    Holy Silence and comprehending it more fully through understanding the role
    silence has played in the Bible, as well as with the Desert Fathers, and in Christian
    spirituality throughout the ages. We will discuss such areas as Benedictine spirituality,
    Hesychasm, centering prayer, and the interface of silence with not only spirituality,
    but also death, love, and the universe itself"—Provided by publisher.
Identifiers: LCCN 2022029074 (print) | LCCN 2022029075 (ebook) | ISBN
    9780761873662 (paperback) | ISBN 9780761873679 (epub)
Subjects: LCSH: Silence—Religious aspects—Christianity.
Classification: LCC BV4509.5 .H534 2022 (print) | LCC BV4509.5 (ebook) | DDC
    248.4/7—dc23/eng/20220815
LC record available at https://lccn.loc.gov/2022029074
LC ebook record available at https://lccn.loc.gov/2022029075

Preach the Gospel always—and if necessary, use words.

—attributed to St. Francis of Assisi

Contents

Chapter 1

Where Are You?

First, let me apologize for all the many "windy words" you are about to read that attempt to describe something as deeply profound, and beyond any one person's understanding as "silence." Because speaking or writing any words at all about silence is most paradoxical, let me also assure you that I am fully aware of the complete irony involved. Please realize, however, that the alternative would be to have a book published with nothing to give you but blank pages or just a book cover with no pages containing any reflective thoughts put into words or images at all.

Silence can signify that we recognize that we are in the presence of someone or something greater than ourselves. It is a word filled with mystery and if you believe in an infinite being or higher power, mystery can be described as the reality of God which is hidden, though still communicated to humankind. Mystery for us then becomes the ground of reality. Therefore, all reality including even the word "silence" is constituted with meaning for each of us. So, for me to reflect on and then choose words that contain some grasp of the meaning of "silence" is both a challenge for me as well as a contradiction for each of us. My hope, however, is that the words I will ultimately be writing, and you will be reading in this book, will give us both a deeper understanding of that mysterious reality we have mutually termed as "silence." Silence can be a call to holiness. That having been said, you will also find that I will frequently use the term "Holy Silence" which is the title of this book. That term when used in the book best describes the essence of that transcendent reality and ultimate mystery which most people simply refer to as "God." It also is the language in which God often speaks to prayerful believers.

Furthermore, I can assure you that without practicing what is called "centering prayer," I wouldn't have any words at all to put on these pages. As we will discuss in a later chapter of this book, centering prayer involves the quieting of our mind, heart, will, and body so that we might listen for what God might be saying to us in the language God often speaks which is silence. Centering prayer can take us to a place beyond any words, thoughts, ideas, images, feelings, or emotions. In praying in this way, we do not seek silence for the sake of being silent, but rather for the sake of listening to God and attempting to hear more clearly. We are not so much seeking to isolate or withdraw ourselves but rather to open ourselves to the presence of God. Thus, silence can become for those of us who practice a daily life of prayer, a pre-condition for hearing God and then hopefully encountering the Lord's presence in both prayer and our daily life.

The center of our being is the sacred space where the Lord meets us in silence. It is far from the surface of who we call our "self." We can sense that we have come to that place when we feel intimacy with God. It is a sense of the heart which no words can express nor can we imagine it in our mind or soul. We are not so much within ourselves as much as being within the silence of the universe with God at our center. Here, there is not conversation, only communion. This hidden union with God is all we really need in any day, and we don't even have to ask God for it. The renunciation of "getting from God" is replaced at our heart center in silent prayer by being given the grace to lose interest in our self and the relinquishing of trying to gain anything for ourselves. It is a spiritual poverty which makes room for God at the center of our being rather than seeking any favors from God. It is only when we empty our "self" that God can fill us with His silence. In doing this, we begin to sense the divine presence of God in all that is personal as well as in all that is universal. There begins communion with God; first in the sacred space within, and then outside our self. St. Augustine said long ago, "I did not find you without, Lord, because I wrongly sought you without who were within."[1] If we can find God within, it can be the beginning of being able to see and find God everywhere, in everyone, and everything.

It is from this centering in silence that any and all of our activity should begin and flow. If we practice this every day, we will essentially become "contemplatives in action." We will no longer see silence as a void to be filled but as an intricate part of vital activity. As said earlier, it is a paradox that God can speak to us in silence. The Lord is always speaking. God first spoke through creation, then through the law and the prophets, then definitively through His Son, Jesus, and ultimately through His Holy Spirit. The Lord, however, will only speak to each of us in prayer in proportion to our awesome wonder of his Holy Silence. The ancient Greek philosopher Socrates told us long ago that, "Wisdom begins in wonder."[2]

Many of the books of the Bible such as Proverbs, Psalms, Wisdom, and Ecclesiastes tell us how silence can be "the eloquence of wisdom."[3] In the same vein, many of the ancient Jewish Rabbis who penned the Talmud have further called silence a "fence around wisdom"[4] and a "blanket over folly." Our being in awe of God's universal love, wisdom, and omnipotence should flow into our love for Him and each other, followed by our desire to listen. Silence removes many of the sinful obstacles on the path to loving. It also then enhances our propensity and willingness to listen for the still small voice of the Lord.

We should always stand ready to defend our Christian faith, but that can often devolve into our simply spouting parroted words. Words can be like nuclear power in that they can be used for good or for bad. They can shape us, form us, and build us up as well as tear us down and sometimes almost destroy us. Even truthful words can sometimes wound us deeply if they are lacking in love. So, before we use our tongue, we need to listen using our heart-center. We need to discern the difference between knowing when to speak or when to be silent. Part of that discernment process involves humbly seeking the Lord through daily prayer, immersing ourselves in Scripture, praying to put on the mind of Christ, and then calling upon the Lord for a share of His wisdom and the stirring of the Holy Spirit within us. Following this, we might attempt to discern the voice of the Lord speaking in silence.

Silence can keep secrets, diffuse anger, avoid disputes, prevent conflicts, and stem a raging tsunami of our own vices. In moments of rising anger inside us, it is often best to refrain from words initially and enter into a brief period of silence first before we speak. We can be fairly certain that if we don't do this and speak out of anger, hurt, frustration, fear, or resentment, the words that roll off our tongue so quickly will often not reflect what the good Lord wants us to speak to another person. We should always want all words that we speak to contribute to another person being built up in Christ or to encourage their well-being.

Temperance and prudence are two of the four cardinal virtues. If it is truly the Holy Spirit speaking through us, we will be expressing the fruit of the Spirit (Gal 5:22). That expression will begin with love, and three of love's facets will be a good measure of peace, patience and self-control. If we are tempted to say something that isn't really going to have a positive influence on others, that is probably a good occasion for us to simply keep silent. This might just be a time where our silence would be perceived as the eloquence of prudence or wisdom. Jesus gives us a warning in Matthew's Gospel:

> A good person brings forth good out of a store of goodness, but an evil person brings forth evil out of a store of evil. I tell you, on the day of judgment people will render an account for every careless word they speak. By your words you will be acquitted, and by your words you will be condemned. (Mt. 12:35–37)

In his beautiful *Ash Wednesday* poem, T. S. Eliot questioned: "Is there enough Silence for the Word to be heard?"[5] Finding the time to be silent can occasionally end up being a struggle for us, but it can be valuable time well spent. The

Bible commends those who are able to maintain silence, to listen attentively and ultimately to keep the peace. On the other hand, the Bible discourages our being silent due to fear or timidity. Courage and justice are the other two of the four cardinal virtues. There will be occasions when remaining silent will not be what the Lord desires of us. We must stand ready to speak truth to power, to address injustices, and courageously defend the weakest, poorest, most vulnerable, or powerless. More will be said on all of this in later chapters. When we speak out, we should always try to have our words be loving, kind, gentle, and gracious. Being aware of God's word in the Bible can empower us to maintain silence or speak out when it is appropriate. Knowing many of the Bible verses on the subject of silence can show us how to find that proper balance. The Bible has much to say about silence. We will find every biblical verse on silence in chapter 4 of this book. One of my favorite scripture verses which advocates silence in the presence of God has always been: "Be still and know that I am God" (Ps. 46:10).[6]

We must make time each day to be "alone together" with God (I recognize the oxymoron here). Entering into a time of silence with the Lord every day can allow God to refresh and restore our souls. There is a quietude of spirit that is necessary for first listening for God and then allowing him to converse with us in the tranquility of our heart-center. We are so used to being interactive and productive each day that it may seem foreign to us to just be alone with the Lord and listen; to do nothing more than that and not take primary charge or assume responsibility for what happens in that time. In that quiet time, the Lord will not just tell us what he wants us to know and to do, but more importantly, the Lord will tell us who He wants us to become.

No professed Christian will ever actually say: "I don't have any time to spend with the Lord." It is our actions, however, which can indicate it. Where and how we spend our time and with whom will show who is important to us in our lives. Who and what we think most about, spend the most time with and love the most, that is indicative of our God. Whether it be time spent with husband, wife, children, relatives, or friends, who would be convinced of their importance in our lives if we didn't spend any quality time with them to show that we love them? Do we spend the majority of our time thinking about things we consider more important than spending time with the Lord? It is impossible to hear the voice of God in silence if we are most often distracted by the false gods of the world. These would include money, power, pleasure and leisure, fame, status or success to name a few. Or have we become self-absorbed with sex, food, alcohol or drugs? Are we pre-occupied with social media or excessive texting or cell phone usage? Anyone or anything that assumes that place of primary importance in our daily lives in many ways can be indicative of our god.

One of the most preeminent Jesuit theologians of our time, the late Karl Rahner, has said: "We each gather rubble around our heart throughout our life. We must allow God to chip away at the rubble each day. Whatever can be taken away from us is never God."[7]

God is never fully absent from us even though we may not be experiencing his presence at times. He is always waiting for us to turn to him, whether it be in word or in silence. Before silence can be our answer, it is a God question. It is the same question God asked Adam when he first walked in the garden of Eden. Our response is not an experience of silence as much as being an experience of grace. Each day, God is looking for us and asking: "Where are you?" (Gn. 3:9).

NOTES

1. Augustine of Hippo, *Confessions*, https://catholic-link.org/11-quotes-saint-augustine-essential-for-our-christian-life/.

2. Socrates, Dialogues of Plato, *Phaedrus*, https://www.reddit.com/r/askphilosophy/comments/2vak3b/trying_to_find_the_source_of_this_quote_is_it/

3. Proverbs 17:27–28, *New American Standard Bible*, United States Conference of Catholic Bishops, The New American Standard version of the Bible will be used for every subsequent biblical verse utilized in this book. See https://bible.usccb.org/.

4. Pirkei Avot, Talmud, *Hassidic Wisdom*, https://www.ou.org/judaism-101/glossary/wisdom/.

5. T. S. Eliot, *Ash Wednesday*, http://famouspoetsandpoems.com/poets/t__s__eliot/poems/15133.

6. Ibid, Ch. 1, f. 3.

7. Karl Rahner, SJ, *Rahner Quotes*, https://www.azquotes.com/author/12033-Karl_Rahner.

Chapter 2

Mary, Icon of Holy Silence

SILENT NIGHT

Silent night, holy night!
All is calm, all is bright.
Round yon Virgin Mother and Child.
Holy infant so tender and mild,
Sleep in heavenly peace,
Sleep in heavenly peace.

Silent night, holy night!
Shepherds quake at the sight.
Glories stream from heaven afar
Heavenly hosts sing Alleluia,
Christ the Savior is born!
Christ the Savior is born

Silent night, holy night!
Son of God love's pure light.
Radiant beams from Thy holy face
With dawn of redeeming grace,
Jesus Lord, at Thy birth
Jesus Lord, at Thy birth

MARY, ICON OF HOLY SILENCE

The Catholic Catechism tells us: "Mary is an icon of the church and in her we can contemplate what the church already is in her mystery on her own 'pilgrimage of faith' and what she will be in the homeland at the end of her journey" (*CC* #972).[1]

An icon can be a window that draws us into silent and prayerful contemplation of God and can make the reality we are visualizing present to us. In a turbulent world filled with noise, chaos, violence, and turmoil, we can often turn our gaze to Mary, the Mother of God, to be our model of tranquility and peace. Furthermore, if we search the Sacred Scriptures, we could not find anyone so completely wrapped in the silence of mystery as the Mother of God. Jesus and Mary always work in concert with one another, and like the Holy Spirit, Mary is always pointing us toward Jesus. The Mother of God does not draw any attention to herself and if silence is the eloquence of wisdom, then Mary becomes for us the Seat of Wisdom. Mary is also a bringer of hope into this despairing world of today. In ancient art she is often depicted holding a dove and an olive branch. As the "Queen of Peace," she bears Jesus in her womb who becomes for us the "Prince of Peace."

As the "Prince of Peace," Jesus will also be a lamb lead to slaughter and our "Agnus Dei." He will suffer and die on the cross and, as prophesied long ago, a sword will pierce Mary's heart (Lk. 2:35). Furthermore, even though God appears to be silent as his Son dies on the cross, he was there—he was actively present and there with his Son on the cross. For this reason, we must learn to prayerfully cultivate interior silence within ourselves so that we can know when God is there, especially when God is silent. We need to be listening, even when it seems that, because of the overwhelming and deafening silence, God may seem completely far away from us, but God is always and eternally present.

St. Ambrose taught: "The mother of God is a type of the church in the order of faith, charity, and the perfect union with Christ."[2] At the foot of the cross of Christ, Mary was close by and must have been silently praying for her son. There she became not only Jesus' mother, but the Apostle John's mother and in the plan of God, our mother as well. Present there with Mary, the Apostle John tells us: "When Jesus saw his mother and the disciple there whom he loved, he said to his mother, 'Woman, behold, your son.' Then, he said to the disciple, 'Behold, your mother.' And from that hour the disciple took her into his home" (Jn. 19:26–27). Beginning at the cross and then at Pentecost with the outpouring of the Holy Spirit, she became the mother of the church. As our gentle mother and icon of the church, Mary can quietly comfort us in our time of need.

In the entire New Testament, Mary's life is cloaked in silence. She barely speaks, and we find her more often listening for God's word to ponder in her heart. Other than her question: "How can this be?" and her "yes" to God through the Angel Gabriel, she is mostly wordless. The first words we have from Mary are these few but her first response is not words, it is silence.

Silence is then followed by attentive listening and subsequently by faith-filled and loving obedience to the will and word of God.

Any questions of her perpetual virginity cannot be addressed by the words of theological argument alone as much as by simple faith. How could the light of the Holy Spirit enter Mary's womb without destroying her virginity? We can only address this metaphorically. We said earlier that an icon is a window and in a natural sense we do know that light can pass silently through a window without destroying or damaging the pane of glass in any way. We are told first by the Apostle Paul in the Bible (1 Cor. 15:46) and subsequently by the angelic doctor of the church, Thomas Aquinas, several times in his writings: "As in the natural, so in the spiritual."[3] For God, all things are possible.

Though often not speaking, Mary is always present to the Lord. Though often wordless, she is never voiceless or passive. She is ever vigilant and waiting on the Lord to speak in the silence of her heart. Through her tranquility, she allows God to speak in her, through her, and with her. Only then will Mary say: "Let it be done to me according to your word" (Lk. 1:38). Her initial choice of silence is representative of her humility, peace, fullness of grace, holiness, and submissive obedience to the word and will of God. Her tranquil, loving, and humble presence speaks not just about who she is, but more importantly, who God is. To God and ultimately for all of Mary's children, her life though hidden, is far from insignificant. Her inner being became the essence of a nurturing silence in that it will express her outward "isness" to the world. The grace-filled essence of Mary's being cannot be fully understood even when using the words "Holy Silence."

In the universal plan of God for the salvation of humankind, it is profoundly ironical yet perfectly fitting that the mother of silence would become the mother of the Word. When anyone speaks, they immediately draw attention to themself. As Jesus' mother and ours, her presence at the wedding in Cana indicates her will for us as her children when Mary says: "Do whatever He tells you" (Jn. 2:5).

Mary's desire has always been to point to the Lord and that all attentiveness be given to her son, Jesus. As her adopted children, the more we get to know Mary as a model of peace and icon of Holy Silence, the more desirous and comfortable we will become with embracing her adoring love. With her as our icon, we can then simply gaze at God in the silent prayer of our heart-center. Our unnecessary thoughts, words, and the images in our mind will give way to opening our hearts to God in prayer and loving adoration. In the noise, turmoil, and chaos existent in the world, we will find with Mary the peace and tranquility we seek in the presence of the serene Spirit of God.

Mary is also considered as an eschatological (last things) icon of all the followers of Christ. In her we contemplate what the Christian church already is in her profound mystery and what the church will be at the end of our pilgrim journey on earth. You cannot separate Mary from Jesus, nor can you separate Mary from the church of God. Her mostly hidden and quiet role will be a key one until the end of time. At Vatican Council II, the *Dogmatic Constitution on the Church* had this to say regarding Mary's role: "By reason of the gift and role of divine maternity, by which she is united with her son, with the redeemer and with His singular graces and functions, the Blessed Virgin is also intimately united with the church."[4]

There are occasions when many of us might feel that our lives are insignificant or that we haven't accomplished much according to the standards of success that the world sets for us. We may even think we are worth little and have no value. We might be hearing the voices of the world saying to us "You've only been a mother who has borne and raised some children." Or: "You've only been a father who supported your family by going to work all your life." Or: "You are just a young person who hasn't had time to do much with your life yet." When we hear those voices of the world, it becomes all the more important for us to draw closer to Mary. As the icon of Holy Silence, she will comfort us as our spiritual and nurturing mother and bring us the peace of knowing that like her, our lives are wrapped in humble prayer and loving obedience. Furthermore, that our lives are hidden in God who values us not only for who we are, but also for who we are becoming in Him. Thomas Merton did not write very much about Mary, the Mother of Jesus Christ. He did, however, write this: "All that has been written about the Virgin Mother of God proves to me that hers is the most hidden of sanctities."[5]

The tranquility, gentleness, and peace of Mary's life, hidden in Holy Silence, is meant for us to first see her as a window into the mystery of God, but she is more than an icon for us to ponder with the eyes of our heart. She is God's mother given to us as our spiritual mother to cherish, honor, celebrate, imitate, and finally to share with all of her other adopted offspring.

HAIL MARY, GENTLE WOMAN

Gentle woman, quiet light,
morning star, so strong and bright,
gentle Mother, peaceful dove,
teach us wisdom; teach us love.
You were chosen by the Father;
you were chosen for the Son.
You were chosen from all women
and for woman, shining one.
Gentle woman, quiet light,
morning star, so strong and bright,

gentle Mother, peaceful dove,
teach us wisdom; teach us love.
Blessed are you among women,
Blessed in turn all women, too.
Blessed they with peaceful spirits.
Blessed they with gentle hearts.[6]

NOTES

1. Catholic Church, Mother of God. In 2nd ed., *Catechism of the Catholic Church* (#972). (Vatican City: Libreria Editrice Vaticana.2012) See also https://www.usccb.org/beliefs-and-teachings/what-we-believe/catechism/catechism-of-the-catholic-church

2. Dogmatic Constitution on the Church, *Lumen Gentium,* Section 3, 21 November 1964. In Vatican Council II: *The Conciliar and Post Conciliar Documents*, edited by Austin Flannery, (Collegeville, MN: Liturgical Press, 1975), pp. 350–426

3. Thomas Aquinas, *Summa Theologica*, Part I, Q. 75; Q. 59), (2002) *NEW ADVENT*. United States. Retrieved from the Library of Congress, https://www.loc.gov/item/lcwaN0008071/.

4. Ibid, Ch. 2, f. 2, Section 8.

5. Thomas Merton, K. Voiles, *The Role of Mary in the Spirituality of Thomas Merton*, http://merton.org/ITMS/Annual/5/Voiles297-310.pdf.

6. Carey Landry, *Hail Mary, Gentle Woman*, http://catholichymn.blogspot.com/2016/08/Hail-Mary-Gentle-Woman.html.

Chapter 3

Hearing, Listening, Discerning, and Obeying

All that the LORD has spoken we will do, and we will be obedient.—Ex. 24:7

SHEMA—HEAR AND OBEY

In the Old Testament, the Hebrew word that translates to "hear or listen," in English is *shema* (pronounced "shmah"). This particular word gives us an excellent example of the difference between Hebrew, which stresses physical action, and the influence of Hellenism which in Greek and Western culture has evolved in time to stress the involvement of mental activity.

In Hebrew, the word *shema* describes not just simply hearing, but also its effects—such as being obedient and doing what is asked. Therefore hearing, if one is listening, should result in responsive action. In fact, almost every place we see the word "obey" in the Bible, it is translated from the word *shema*. *Shema* is also the name of a pledge of allegiance that observant Jews until this day have recited every morning and evening. This would include Jesus of Nazareth. It is the first word of the first line, "Hear (*Shema*), O Israel! The LORD is our God, the LORD alone. You shall love the LORD your God with all your heart and with all your soul and with all your might" (Dt. 6:4–5).[1] By reciting this, an observant Jew is reminded of their commitment to love God, to obey God, and to be dedicated to doing God's will. Many Jews teach their children the *shema* as soon as they learn how to talk. It is central to the Jewish persons' understanding of their commitment to the God of Israel. In essence then, the word *shema* to the observant Jew means essentially, not just to hear, but to listen and obey!

13

This gives us a clue as to why Jesus says, "He who has ears to hear, let him hear!" (Mt. 11:15, Mk. 4). He is calling us to put his words into action, not just listen. He wants us to be doers of the word, and not hearers only (Jm. 1:22). We as Westerners put all our stress on what is in our minds and tend to consider action as "dead works." Hebrews understood that we have not truly put what we have heard into our hearts until it transforms our lives. "Obey" and "hear," both come from the same root verb; in the ancient Hebrew languages, that being, *shema*. Most English words, however, are derived from Latin. In the Latin, we find a similarity in the root verb as well. The Latin word, "obedire" (ob (toward) + audire (listening) renders the Latin translation "toward listening." Thus, it can also be similarly translated as "hear" and "obey."

Furthermore, it should be understood that there is a marked difference between "hearing" and "listening." In our culture, listening is a mental activity. Hearing is one of the five human senses. It pertains to our ear performing its function. The eardrum transfers the vibration of sound waves to the tiny bones in the inner ear and nerves carry these signals to the brain. The brain then processes it and interprets it. Ultimately, we perceive the sound and react to it. If we are not hearing-impaired, hearing happens. On the other hand, listening involves conscious choice. It is an active process that makes obedience ultimately possible.

Silence has the ability to enhance both our natural hearing and the active listening process which can ultimately result in our obedience to God. We need to discern the difference between knowing when to speak or when to be silent. Part of that discernment process involves humbly seeking the Lord through prayer, immersing ourselves in Scripture, and then calling upon the Lord for a share in his wisdom and discernment as we listen for the Lord who will speak in the silence of our hearts. Silence enhances our ability to listen, hear, discern, and obey.

There are many occasions in our lives when our heart is too heavily burdened, our soul too overwhelmed with grief, or our mind is too confused to put our prayer to God into any form of words. Wordlessness might be the only way we can speak to God. Especially during these difficult times, it is so important to just enter into the silence and wait patiently for God to speak. God hears our prayer when we can't put all that is going on in our lives into words. At those times, deep can speak to deep in the silence of the center of our being. The Apostle Paul confirms this in the New Testament Book of Romans: "The Spirit too comes to the aid of our weakness; for we do not know how to pray as we ought, but the Spirit itself intercedes with inexpressible groanings. And the one who searches hearts knows the intention of the Spirit, because it intercedes for the holy ones according to God's will" (Rom. 8:26–27).

To both, hear and obey, we must first enter into a time of prayer in order that we might listen and discern what might be the will of God for our lives. We cannot obey if we are not silent enough to listen and listening might help us to discern and subsequently to obey. This is true on both a physical level as well as a spiritual one as our body must be as present, tranquil, and calm as our spirit.

The discernment process is a critical one to the entire sequence. Discernment ultimately involves decision making and choices as well as prudent perception. As much as possible any Christian should want the choice to be both our choice and God's; therefore, guidance by the Holy Spirit is absolutely necessary. So, discernment can be described as the process by which we decide who God wants us to be and what God wills us to do now and in the future. Only in the silence of prayer can we attempt to discern what the Lord might be saying to us about the various choices. How can we hear and obey the Lord unless we attempt to discern the Lord's will for us? Furthermore, how can discernment be possible unless we listen in the silence of our heart-center?

In Ignatian spirituality there are some various steps we might consider utilizing to discern God's will in any situation, such as identifying an issue before us we need to discern, taking the time to pray about it in silence, discerning the alternative choices and avoiding any pre-judgement. Additionally, we should ask for the guidance of the Holy Spirit, while discussing it with a mentor or in a prayerful community as we identify the pros and cons. Then we can make a decision based on the choices, while praying again in silence for openness to what is believed to be God's will. Consequently, we can attempt to live with that decision for a time, while testing it and praying in silence for the grace to obey what we believe is then in harmony with the mind of Christ.[2]

Meditating on Sacred Scripture can link our heart with our thought processes and what comes into our mind and eventually out of our mouth. The Gospels confirm this as they tell us: "From the fullness of the heart the mouth speaks" (Mt. 12:34, Lk. 6:45). This is a metaphor that implies that only when our heart enters into the silence of God are we then in a place to listen and hear. Only when we receive God's word in silence with an open heart, then and only then can we ultimately be in a position to discern and ultimately to hear and obey. Just as God understands us without our needing to say anything, one day when God makes us all one with Him, we will understand each other in perfect silence without saying anything at all. This often happens now in the case of two lovers where words are often unnecessary.

The sequence can be envisioned as a complete circle of love. Love should lead us to the awesome wonder of God, awesome wonder to wisdom, wisdom should guide us into prayer. Prayer should lead us into silence where God can speak to us. Silence can be a path toward our ability to listen to God.

Listening can then lead to discernment and discernment ultimately to hearing and obeying. Obedience will then lead us back to greater love for God and one another.

Learning to be silent and spending our precious and valuable time with the Lord is one of the greatest challenges any Christian faces today who desires to enter into an experience of true intimacy with the risen Lord. It is also one of the greatest gifts we can give to ourselves. Loving God and loving another involves our free will. What follows is that any life lived in love is about having the freedom to make wise choices. Most Christians would not want to make any major choice that didn't first include asking for the guidance of the Holy Spirit in the silence of our hearts. So, hearing, listening, discerning, and obeying often involves going back to the basics. Returning to the basics often involves first, our communing with God's Spirit in Holy Silence.

NOTES

1. "The Shema," Ibid, Ch. 1, f. 3.

2. Ignatius, of Loyola, Saint, *The Spiritual Exercises of St. Ignatius Loyola*: a new translation by Elisabeth Meier Tetlow. (Lanham, MD: University Press of America, 1987), pp. 1–142. see also https://www.ignatianspirituality.com/,https://www.loyolapress.com/catholic-resources/ignatian-spirituality/examen-and-ignatian-prayer/what-are-the-spiritual-exercises-of-saint-ignatius/.

Chapter 4

The Bible and Silence

Ignorance of the Scriptures is ignorance of Christ.—St. Jerome[1]

LECTIO DIVINA

The Scriptures hold the Divine Word of God. They are an invitation to know and love God more fully in the silence of our heart. They contain the power of the Holy Spirit which can stir our hearts and develop and refine our intelligence through grace. This should cause us to recognize that God and His Word are the source and end of all love and knowledge.

In Christianity, as an institutionalized world religion, *Lectio Divina* (Divine Reading) is a traditional monastic practice which encompasses the reading of Sacred Scripture combined with meditation and silent prayer. This practice is intended to promote intimate communion with God and to increase the knowledge of God's word. It does not treat Scripture as a series of biblical books and several texts to be studied as much as the living Word of God to pray with and contemplate in silence. This practice of *Lectio Divina* involves four basic steps:

1. The Reading (Lectio)
   This first step is the reading of Scripture. The preparation for the reading should begin with a quieted and calm state of mind and being. A biblical reference for preparation could be Psalm 46:10: "Be still and know that I am God." One should be sitting in peace and tranquility while prayerfully inviting the Holy Spirit to guide the reading of the Scripture that will follow. The preparation prior to the reading should ask the Holy Spirit to open the heart to find God's presence in the Scripture passage about to be read. Following the preparation begins the

17

gradual reading of a Scriptural passage several times. In the Benedictine approach the passage is traditionally read four times slowly, silently, and reflectively. Each time one should attempt to see the Scripture passage differently and approach its intended meaning from various perspectives.

2. The Meditation

   Although Lectio Divina involves the reading of Scripture, it is more a practice of listening in silence to the heart-message of the Scripture. This message is delivered by the Holy Spirit alive within the words of Scripture and also living within the baptized Christian. The practice of *Lectio Divina* ultimately seeks intimate communion with God through our interiorization of God's living word contained in Sacred Scripture. When one reads the passage, we should not try initially to assign a meaning to it but to wait silently for the action of the Holy Spirit to illuminate the mind. The emphasis should not be on an analysis of the Scripture text as much as asking the Lord to open our hearts and allow the Holy Spirit to inspire a meaning for it. Thus, our focus in meditation should be on allowing ourselves to be moved toward a closer communion with the Holy Spirit in prayerful silence rather than a thoughtful biblical analysis or an exegesis of the Scripture passage.

3. The Prayer

   The Vatican II Constitution titled "The Word of God" (*Dei Verbum*) endorsed *Lectio Divina* for a broader Christian audience as well as for its use in monastic settings where the importance of silent prayer in conjunction with Scripture reading is typically recommended.[2] When we read Scripture quietly and prayerfully, we can listen for God's voice and have an opportunity to hear Him as He speaks to us through his Divine Word. For Scripture tells us: "Thy Word is a lamp to my feet and a light to my path" (Ps. 119:105).

4. The Contemplation

   Contemplation can begin to occur whenever prayer expresses a heart-felt love for God. Contemplative prayer is essentially "the hearing of the Word of God with a willingness to obey." It can sometimes simply be called "silent love." The biblical words we read in this kind of prayer are only used to kindle the fire of love. The kindling will disappear as the fire gets going. In the ensuing mutual communion, the Holy Spirit in contemplative prayer allows us the grace to experience mystical and intimate union with God. What follows are several Old Testament and New Testament biblical texts for the practice of silent prayerful reading. Let us attempt to utilize the ancient monastic practice of *Lectio Divina* and its four steps as we begin to read the Word of God, then meditate, contemplate, and reflect on the Word of God as we invite the Holy Spirit to join us in this "silent love."

Come Holy Spirit, fill the hearts of your faithful and kindle in them the fire of your love. Send forth your Spirit and they shall be created. And You shall renew the face of the earth.

OLD TESTAMENT

Wisdom Books

Proverbs 10:19
When there are many words,
transgression is unavoidable,
But he who stays silent is wise.

Proverbs 11:12
He who despises his neighbor lacks sense,
But a man of understanding keeps silent.

Proverbs 17:28
Even a fool, when he keeps silent,
is considered wise.
When he closes his lips,
he is considered prudent.

Proverbs 18:21
Death and life are in the power of the tongue;
those who choose one shall eat its fruit.

Proverbs 24:7
Wise words are beyond fools' reach,
in the assembly they are silent.

Proverbs 29:11
A fool gives full vent to his spirit,
but a wise man silently holds it back.

Wisdom 8:9–12
So, I determined to take wisdom to live with me,
knowing that she would be my counselor while all was well,
and my comfort in care and grief.
Because of her I have glory among the multitudes,
and esteem from the elders, though I am but a youth.
I shall become keen in judgment,
and shall be a marvel before rulers.
They will wait while I am silent
and listen when I speak;

and when I shall speak the more,
they will put their hands upon their mouths.

Sirach 13:23
When the rich speak all are silent,
their wisdom people extol to the clouds.
When the poor speak people say: "Who is that?"
If they stumble, people knock them down.

Sirach 20:5–7
One is silent and is thought wise;
another, for being talkative, is disliked.
One is silent, having nothing to say;
another is silent, biding his time.
The wise remain silent till the right time comes,
but a boasting fool misses the proper time.

Sirach 20:29–31
Favors and gifts blind the eyes;
like a muzzle over the mouth
they silence reproofs.
Hidden wisdom and unseen treasure—
what value has either?
Better are those who hide their folly
than those who hide their wisdom.

Ecclesiastes 3:1, 7
There is an appointed time for everything,
and a time for every affair under the heavens. . . .
A time to be silent and a time to speak.

Ecclesiastes 9:17
The words of the wise are heard in silence,
more than the cry of those who rule among fools.

Job 2:13
Then they sat down on the ground with him
for seven days and seven nights in silence
for they saw that his pain was very great.

Job 3:13
For now, should I have
lain still and been silent,

I should have slept:
then had I been at rest.

Job 3:26
I was not in safety,
neither had I rest,
neither was I silent;
yet trouble came.

Job 4:16
It stood still, but I could not discern its appearance.
A form was before my eyes;
there was silence, then I heard a voice.

Job 6:24
Teach me, and I will be silent;
make me understand how I have erred.

Job 7:11
Therefore, I will not keep silent.
I will speak in the anguish of my spirit.
I will complain in the bitterness of my soul.

Job 13:5
O that you would be completely silent,
And that it would become your wisdom!

Job 13:13
Be silent!
Let me alone that I may speak,
no matter what happens to me.

Job 21:23
One dies in his full strength,
being wholly at ease and silent.

Job 29:7–10
When I went out to the gate of the city,
When I took my seat in the square,
The young men saw me and hid themselves,
And the old men arose and stood.
The princes were silent
And put their hands on their mouths.

Job 29:21
Men listened to me and waited
and kept silence for my counsel.

Job 31:34
Because I stood in great fear of the multitude,
and the contempt of families terrified me,
so that I kept silence, and did not go out of doors—

Job 33:31–33
Pay attention, O Job, listen to me;
Keep silent and let me speak.
Then if you have anything to say, answer me;
Speak, for I desire to justify you.
If not, listen to me;
Keep silent, and I will teach you wisdom.

The Psalms

Psalm 22:2–3
My God, my God, why have you abandoned me?
Why so far from my call for help,
from my cries of anguish?
My God, I call by day, but you are silent;
by night, but I have no relief.

Psalm 28:1
To You, O Lord, I call;
My rock, do not be deaf to me,
For if You are silent to me,
I will become like those who go down to the pit.

Psalm 30:12–13
You changed my mourning into dancing;
you took off my sackcloth
and clothed me with gladness.
So that my glory may praise you
and not be silent.

Psalm 31:18
Let the lying lips be silent,
which speak insolently against
the righteous in pride and contempt.

Psalm 32:3
For when I kept silent,

my bones wasted away
through my groaning all day long.

Psalm 35:22
You have seen, O Lord; be not silent!
O Lord, be not far from me!

Psalm 37:7
Be silent before the Lord
and wait patiently for him;
fret not yourself over
the one who prospers in his way,
over the man who carries out evil devices!

Psalm 39:2
I was mute and silent;
I held my peace to no avail,
and my distress grew worse.

Psalm 39:12
"Hear my prayer, O Lord, and give ear to my cry;
Do not be silent at my tears;
For I am a stranger with You,
A sojourner like all my fathers.

Psalm 46:10
Be still and know that I am God.

Psalm 50:3
May our God come and not keep silence;
Fire devours before Him,
And it is very tempestuous around Him.

Psalm 50:21
These things you have done, and I have been silent;
you thought that I was one like yourself.

Psalm 62:5
For God alone, O my soul, wait in silence,
for my hope is from him.

Psalm 83:1
O God, do not keep silence;
do not hold your peace or be still, O God!

Psalm 94:17
If the Lord had not been my help,
my soul would soon have lived in the land of silence.

Psalm 107:29–30
He hushed the storm to silence,
the waves of the sea were stilled.
They rejoiced that the sea grew calm,
that God brought them to the harbor they longed for.

Psalm 107:42
The upright see it and are glad;
But all unrighteousness is silent.

Psalm 109:1
O God of my praise,
Do not be silent!

Psalm 115:17
The dead do not praise the Lord,
nor do any who go down into silence.

Psalm 131:1–3
LORD, my heart is not proud;
nor are my eyes haughty.
I do not busy myself with great matters,
with things too sublime for me.
Rather, I have silenced my soul,
Like a weaned child to its mother,
weaned is my soul.
Israel, hope in the LORD,
now and forever.

Psalm 141:3
Set a guard, O Lord,
To silence my mouth;
keep watch over the door of my lips.

Historical Books

Genesis 24:21
Meanwhile, the man was gazing at her in silence,
to know whether the Lord
had made his journey successful or not.

Exodus 14:14
The Lord will fight for you while you keep silent.

Leviticus 5:2
If anyone sins in that he hears a public adjuration to testify,
and though he is a witness,
whether he has seen or come to know the matter,
yet is silent, he shall bear his iniquity.

Deuteronomy 27:9
Moses, with the levitical priests,
then said to all Israel:
Be silent, Israel, and listen!
This day you have become
the people of the LORD, your God.

Joshua 6:10
But Joshua commanded the people, saying,
"You shall not shout nor let your voice be heard.
Let your mouth be silent,
until the day I tell you, 'Shout!'
Then you shall shout!"

2 Kings 2:3
Then the sons of the prophets who were at Bethel
came out to Elisha and said to him,
"Do you know that the Lord
will take away your master from over you today?"
And he said, "Yes, I know; be silent."

Judges 3:19
But he himself turned back
at the idols near Gilgal and said,
"I have a secret message for you, O king."
And he commanded, "Silence."
And all his attendants went out from his presence.

Judges 18:19
They said to him, "Be silent,
put your hand over your mouth and come with us."

1 Samuel 1:13
Hannah was praying silently;
though her lips were moving,
her voice could not be heard.

1 Samuel 2:9
He guards the footsteps of his faithful ones,
but the wicked shall perish in silence;
for not by strength does one prevail.

1 Samuel 10:27
But certain worthless men said,
"How can this one deliver us?"
And they despised him
and did not bring him any present.
But he kept silent.

Prophetic Books

Lamentations 2:10
The elders of the daughter of Zion
sit on the ground in silence;
they have thrown dust on their heads and put on sackcloth.

Lamentations 3:26
It is good that one should wait silently
for the salvation of the Lord.

Isaiah 14:7
The whole earth is at rest and is silent:
they break forth into singing.

Isaiah 18:4
When the trumpet blows, listen!
For thus says the LORD to me:
I will be silent,
looking on from where I dwell,

Isaiah 25:5
Like heat in drought,
You subdue the uproar of aliens;
Like heat by the shadow of a cloud,
the song of the ruthless is silenced.

Isaiah 30:15
For thus said the Lord God,
the Holy One of Israel,
"In returning and rest you shall be saved;
in silence and in trust shall be your strength."

Isaiah 36:21
But they remained silent
and did not answer at all,
for the king's command was,
"Do not answer him."

Isaiah 41:1
Listen to me in silence, O coastlands;
let the peoples renew their strength;
let them approach, then let them speak;
let us together draw near for judgment.

Isaiah 42:14
I have kept silent for a long time,
I have kept still and restrained Myself.
Now like a woman in labor I will groan,
I will both gasp and pant.

Isaiah 47:5
Sit in silence, and go into darkness,
O daughter of the Chaldeans;
for you shall no more be called the mistress of kingdoms.

Isaiah 53:7
He was oppressed and He was afflicted,
Yet He did not open His mouth;
Like a lamb that is led to slaughter,
And like a sheep that is silent before its shearers,
So, He did not open His mouth.

Isaiah 62:1
For Zion's sake I will not keep silent,
And for Jerusalem's sake I will not keep quiet,
Until her righteousness goes forth like brightness,
And her salvation like a torch that is burning.

Isaiah 62:6
On your walls, O Jerusalem, I have set watchmen;
all the day and all the night they shall never be silent.

Isaiah 64:12
Will You restrain Yourself at these things, O Lord?
Will You keep silent and afflict us beyond measure?

Isaiah 65:6–7
Behold, it is written before Me,
I will not keep silent, but I will repay;

Jeremiah 48:2
There is praise for Moab no longer;
In Heshbon they have devised calamity against her:
"Come and let us cut her off from being a nation!"
You too, Madmen, will be silenced;
The sword will follow after you.

Jeremiah 49:23
Concerning Damascus.
Hamath and Arpad are shamed,
for they have heard bad news;
Anxious, they surge like the sea
which cannot be silent.

Daniel 10:13–16
I came to make you understand
what shall happen to your people in the last days;
for there is yet a vision concerning those days.
While he was speaking thus to me,
I fell forward and kept silent.

Habakkuk 1:13
Your eyes are too pure to approve evil,
and You cannot look on wickedness with favor.
Why do You look with favor
on those who deal treacherously?
Why are You silent when the wicked swallow up
Those more righteous than they?

Habakkuk 2:20
But the Lord is in His holy temple.
Let all the earth be silent before Him

Ezekiel 24:17
Groan silently;
make no mourning for the dead.
Bind on your turban
and put your shoes on your feet,
and do not cover your mustache
and do not eat the bread of men.

Ezekiel 26:13
So, I will silence
the sound of your songs,
and the sound of your harps
will be heard no more.

Amos 5:13
Therefore at such a time
the wise person keeps silent,
for it is an evil time.

Amos 8:3
"The songs of the temple shall become wailings in that day,"
declares the Lord God.
"So many dead bodies!"
"They are thrown everywhere!" "Silence!"

Zephaniah 1:7
Be silent before the Lord God!
For the day of the Lord is near,
For the Lord has prepared a sacrifice,
He has consecrated His guests.

Zechariah 2:17
Silence, all people,
in the presence of the LORD,
who stirs forth from his holy dwelling.

New Testament

Matthew 22:34
But when the Pharisees heard that
Jesus had silenced the Sadducees,
they gathered themselves together.

Matthew 26:62–63
But Jesus kept silent.
And the high priest said to Him,
"I adjure You by the living God,
that You tell us whether
You are the Christ, the Son of God."

Mark 1:23–25
In their synagogue was a man with an unclean spirit;
he cried out, "What have you to do with us, Jesus of Nazareth?
Have you come to destroy us?

I know who you are—the Holy One of God!"
Jesus rebuked him and said, "Silence! Come out of him!"

Mark 3:4
And He said to them,
"Is it lawful to do good
or to do harm on the Sabbath,
to save a life or to kill?"
But they kept silent.

Mark 4: 37–40
A violent squall came up
and waves were breaking over the boat,
so that it was already filling up.
Jesus was in the stern, asleep on a cushion.
They woke him and said to him,
"Teacher, do you not care that we are perishing?"
He woke up, rebuked the wind, and said to the sea,
"Silence! Be still!"
The wind ceased and there was great calm.

Mark 10:48
Many were sternly telling him to be silent,
but he kept crying out all the more,
"Son of David, have mercy on me!"

Mark 14:61
But He kept silent and did not answer.
Again, the high priest was questioning Him,
and saying to Him,
"Are You the Christ, the Son of the Blessed One?"

Mark 15:4–5
Then Pilate questioned Him again,
saying, "Do You not answer?
See how many charges they bring against You!"
But Jesus was silent;
so Pilate was amazed.

Luke 1:20
But now you will be silent and unable to talk
until the day these things take place,
because you did not believe my words,
which will be fulfilled at their proper time.

Luke 9:36
And when the voice had spoken,
Jesus was found alone.
And they kept silent,
and reported to no one in those days
any of the things which they had seen.

Luke 14:4
But they kept silent;
so he took the man
and, after he had healed him,
dismissed him.

Luke 19:40
He said in reply,
"I tell you, if they keep silent,
the stones will cry out!"

Luke 20:26
And they were unable to catch Him
in a saying in the presence of the people;
and being amazed at His answer,
they became silent.

John 19:9
and he entered into the Praetorium again
and said to Jesus,
"Where are You from?"
But Jesus was silent.

Acts 4:14
And seeing the man who had been healed
standing with them, they were silent.

Acts 8:32
Now the passage of Scripture which he was reading was this:
"He was led as a sheep to slaughter;
And as a lamb before its shearer is silent,
So, He does not open His mouth."

Acts 12:17
Peter motioned to them
with his hand to be silent
and explained how the Lord
had led him out of the prison,

Acts 15:12
All the people kept silent,
and they were listening
to Barnabas and Paul
as they were relating
what signs and wonders
God had done through them
among the Gentiles.

Acts 18:9–10
One night in a vision
the Lord said to Paul,
"Do not be afraid.
Go on speaking,
and do not be silent,
for I am with you."

Acts 21:40
Paul stood on the steps
and motioned with his hand to the people;
and when all were silent
he addressed them in Hebrew.

Acts 22:2
When they heard Paul
addressing them in Hebrew
they became all the more silent.

Romans 3:19
Now we know that whatever the Law says,
it speaks to those who are under the Law,
so that every mouth may be silenced
and all the world may become accountable to God.

1 Corinthians 13:8
Love never fails.
If there are prophecies,
they will be brought to nothing;
if tongues, they will be silent;
if knowledge, it will be brought to nothing.

1 Corinthians 14:28
But if there is no one to interpret,
let each of them keep silent in church
and speak to himself and to God.

1 Corinthians 14:34–35
The women should keep silent in the churches
For they are not permitted to speak,
but should be in submission, as the Law also says.
If there is anything they desire to learn,
let them ask their husbands at home.
For it is shameful for a woman to speak in church.

1 Peter 2:15
For this is the will of God,
that by doing good
you should put to silence
the ignorance of foolish people.

1 Peter 4:7
Remain silent so that you will be able to pray.

1 Timothy 2:11–14
Let a woman learn silently
with all submissiveness.

Revelation 8:1
When the Lamb broke the seventh seal,
there was silence in heaven for about half an hour.[3]

NOTES

1. St. Jerome, https://www.azquotes.com/author/7422-St_Jerome.
2. Ibid, Ch. 2, f. 2, *Dei Verbum*.
3. Ibid, Ch. 1, f. 3.

Chapter 5

The Desert Fathers and Silence

If one cannot understand my silence, he will never understand my words.—Abba Pambo

The Desert Fathers (abbas) and Mothers (ammas) were monks and hermits who fled to the Egyptian desert to escape Christian persecution. They lived alone in solitary caves or cells and were part of a broader Christian community or coenobium (common life) which met weekly to celebrate the Eucharist. They chose to live lives of silent prayer, work, and asceticism rather than face martyrdom under the rule of brutal and merciless Roman emperors. Their lives formed the basis of what would later become widespread Christian Monasticism.

Their traditional oral sayings were eventually compiled into a collection which was titled *The Apophthegmata Patrum* (The Sayings of the Desert Fathers). The most notable of the Desert Fathers was Anthony the Great, who upon hearing the Gospel read one day sold all his possessions. He abandoned his comfortable lifestyle to live an ascetic life of silent prayer and solitude in the desert. Many of these twelve hundred sayings in the total composition go back to the first few centuries of the fledgling Christian church. They date from the 3rd to the 5th centuries A.D. and influenced many early Christian theologians, most notably St. Jerome and St. Augustine. In their entirety, they were originally spoken by many Desert Fathers and principally by three Desert Mothers. Through the example of their way of life and steadfast praying these early Christian monks and hermits sought to achieve what was called "hesychia" or an inner silence which produced calmness, tranquility, and the profound peace of Christ within. Hesychasm as a formal practice of silent prayer did not become an organized movement until the 14th century and will be discussed in further detail in chapter 10 of this book.

The following forty-two selected wisdom sayings strictly related to silence were taken from the broader compilations of several different translations listed at the end of this chapter. I could find no sayings on silence among the three notable Desert Mothers, Syncletica, Sarah, and Theodora. However, when you read and reflect on their overall sayings in the composition, one finds that the sayings of the Desert Mothers were certainly filled with as much wisdom as the Desert Fathers. And it is certainly not to say that silence was not practiced by the Desert Mothers, as it was most probably a part of their daily prayer-filled lives of asceticism. They simply did not record any wisdom sayings on the subject of silence.

The Sayings of the Desert Fathers on Silence/*from Apophthegmata Patrum* (L.)

1. When he was dying, Abba Pambo said: "From the time that I came into this solitude and built my cell and dwelt in it, I cannot remember eating any food that I have not earned with my own hands, nor speaking any word that I have been sorry for until now. And so I go to the Lord, as one who has not yet begun to serve God. For Abba Arsenius, this was a rule for the whole of life: 'Be solitary, be silent, and be at peace.'"

2. Abba Pambo asked Abba Anthony, "What ought I to do?" and the old man said to him, "Do not trust in your own righteousness, do not worry about the past, but control your tongue and your stomach."

3. Three Fathers used to go and visit blessed Anthony every year and two of them used to discuss their thoughts and the salvation of their souls with him, but the third always remained silent and did not ask him anything. After a long time, Abba Anthony said to him, "You often come here to see me, but you never ask me anything," and the other replied, "It is enough for me to see you, Father."

4. Some say of Saint Anthony that he was "Spirit-borne," that is, carried along by the Holy Spirit, but he would never speak of this to men. Such men see what is happening in the world, as well as knowing what is going to happen.

5. While still living in the palace, Abba Arsenius prayed to God in these words, "Lord, lead me in the way of salvation." And a voice came saying to him, "Arsenius, flee from men and you will be saved." Having withdrawn to the solitary life he made the same prayer again and he heard a voice saying to him, "Arsenius, flee, be silent, pray always, for these are the source of sinlessness."

6. One day Abba Arsenius came to a place where there were reeds blowing in the wind. The old man said to the brothers, "What is this movement?" They said, "Some reeds." Then the old man said to them, "When one who is living in silent prayer hears the song of a little sparrow, his heart no longer experiences the same peace. How much worse it is when you hear the movement of those reeds."

7. When Abba Arsenius was at the point of death, his disciples were troubled. He said to them, "The time has not yet come; when it comes, I will tell you." The old man used to say to himself, "Arsenius, why have you left the world? I have often repented of having spoken, but never of having been silent." When his death drew near, the brethren saw him weeping and they said to him, "Truly, Father, are you also afraid?" "Indeed," he answered them, "the fear which is mine at this hour has been with me ever since I became a monk." Upon this he fell asleep.

8. Abba Peter, the disciple of Abba Lot, said, "One day when I was in Abba Agathon's cell, a brother came in and said to him, 'I want to live with the brethren; tell me how to dwell with them.'" The old man answered him, "All the days of your life keep the frame of mind of the stranger which you have on the first day you join them, so as not to become too familiar with them." The Abba Macarius asked, "And what does this familiarity produce?" The old man replied, "It is like a strong, burning wind, each time it arises everything flies swept before it, and it destroys the fruit of the trees." So, Abba Macarius said, "Is speaking too freely really as bad as all that?" Abba Agathon said, "No passion is worse than an uncontrolled tongue because it is the mother of all the passions."

9. It was said of Abba Agathon that for three years he lived with a stone in his mouth, until he had learned to keep silence.

10. It was said of Abba Agathon and of Abba Amoun that, when they had anything to sell, they would name the price just once and silently accept what was given them in peace. Just as when they wished to buy something, they gave the price they were asked in silence and took the object adding no further word.

11. Abba Anthony predicted that this Abba Ammonas would make progress in the fear of God. He led him outside his cell, and showing him a stone, said to him, "Hurt this stone, and beat it." He did so. Then Anthony asked him, "Has the stone said anything?" He replied, "No." Then Anthony said, "You too will be able to do that," and that is what happened.

12. It was said of Abba Amoun that a very small quantity of wheat every two months was sufficient for him. Now he went to find Abba Poemen and said to him, "When I go to my neighbor's cell, or when he comes to mine for some need or other, we are afraid of entering into conversation, for fear of slipping into worldly subjects." The old man replied, "You are right, for young men need to be watchful." Then Abba Amoun continued, "But the old men, what do they do?" He replied, "The old men who have advanced in virtue, have nothing in them that is worldly; there is nothing worldly in their mouths of which they could speak." "But," Amoun replied, "When I am obliged to speak to my neighbor, do you prefer me to speak of the Scriptures or of the sayings of the Fathers?" The old man answered him, "If you can't be silent, you had better talk about the sayings of the Fathers than about the Scriptures; it is not so dangerous."

13. Then Abba Anoub said to Abba Poemen, "For love's sake do this: let each of us live in quietness, each one by himself, without meeting one another the whole week." Abba Poemen replied, "We will do as you wish." So, they did this. Now there was in the temple a statue of stone. When he woke up in the morning, Abba Anoub threw stones at the face of the statue, and in the evening he said to it, "Forgive me." During the whole week he did this. On Saturday they came together, and Abba Poemen said to Abba Anoub, "Abba, I have seen you during the whole week throwing stones at the face of the statue and kneeling to ask it to forgive you. Does a believer act thus?" The old man answered him, "I did this for your sake. When you saw me throwing stones at the face of the statue, did it speak, or did it become angry?" Abba Poemen said, "No." "Or again, when I bent down in penitence, was it moved, and did it say, 'I will not forgive you?'" Again, Abba Poemen answered, "No." Then the old man resumed, "Now we are seven brethren; if you wish us to live together, let us be like this statue, which is not moved whether one beats it or whether one flatters it."

14. Abba Andrew said, "These three things are appropriate for a monk: exile, poverty, and endurance in silence."

15. A brother who shared a lodging with other brothers asked Abba Bessarion, "What should I do?" The old man replied, "Keep silence and do not compare yourself with others."

16. The same old man said, "The Canaanite woman cries out, and she is heard (Matt. 15); the woman with the issue of blood is silent, and she is

called blessed (Lk. 8); the pharisee speaks, and he is condemned (Matt. 9); the publican does not open his mouth, and he is heard (Lk. 18)."

17. The same abba said, "The righteous sin through their mouths, but the ungodly sin in their whole bodies. This is why David sings; 'Set, O Lord, a watch before my mouth and keep the door of my lips." (Ps. 141:3). And again, 'I will take heed to my ways that I do not sin with my tongue'" (Ps. 39:1).

18. Abba Evagrius said, "Sit in your cell, collecting your thoughts. Remember the day of your death. See then what the death of your body will be; let your spirit be heavy, take pains, condemn the vanity of the world, so as to be able to live always in the peace you have in view without weakening. Remember also what happens in hell and think about the state of the souls down there, their painful silence, their most bitter groanings, their fear, their strife, their waiting. Think of their grief without end and the tears their souls shed eternally. But keep the day of resurrection and of presentation to God in remembrance also."

19. A brother came to Abba Theodore and spent three days begging him to say a word to him without getting any reply. So, he went away grieved. Then the old man's disciple said to him, "Abba, why did you not say a word to him? See, he has gone away grieved." The old man said to him, "I did not speak to him, for he is a trafficker who seeks to glorify himself through the words of others."

20. One day Abba Theodore was entertaining himself with the brethren. While they were eating, they drank their cups with respect, but in silence, without even saying "pardon." So, Abba Theodore said, "The monks have lost their manners and do not say, 'pardon.'"

21. The same Abba Theophilus, the archbishop, came to Scetis one day. The brethren who were assembled said to Abba Pambo, "Say something to the archbishop, so that he may be edified." The old man said to them, "If he is not edified by my silence, he will not be edified by my speech."

22. Abba John said, 'Who sold Joseph?" A brother replied saying, "It was his brethren." The old man said to him, "No, it was his humility which sold him, because he could have said, 'I am their brother' and have objected, but, because he kept silence, he sold himself by his humility. It is also his humility which set him up as chief in Egypt."

23. A brother asked Abba Isidore, "Why are the demons so frightened of you?" The old man said to him, "Because I have practiced asceticism since the day I became a monk, and not allowed anger to reach my lips."

24. Abba Isidore of Pelusia said, "To live without speaking is better than to speak without living. For the former who lives rightly does good even by his silence, but the latter does no good even when he speaks. When words and life correspond to one another they are together the whole of philosophy."

25. Abba Isaac said, "When I was younger, I lived with Abba Cronius. He would never tell me to do any work, although he was old and tremulous; but he himself got up and offered food to me and to everyone. Then I lived with Abba Theodore of Pherme and he did not tell me to do anything either, but he himself set the table and said to me, 'Brother, if you want to, come and eat.' I replied, 'I have come to you to help you, why do you never tell me to do anything?' But the old man gave me no reply whatever. So, I went to tell the old men. They came and said to him, 'Abba, the brother has come to your holiness in order to help you. Why do you never tell him to do anything?' The old man said to them, 'Am I a cenobite, that I should give him orders? As far as I am concerned, I do not tell him anything, but if he wishes he can do what he sees me doing.' From that moment I took the initiative and did what the old man was about to do. As for him, what he did, he did in silence; so, he taught me to work in silence."

26. Abba James said, "We do not need words only, for, at the present time, there are many words among men, but we need works, for this is what is required, not words which do not bear fruit."

27. Abba Carion said, "I have labored much harder than my son Zacharias and yet I have not attained to his measure in humility and silence."

28. Another day when a council was being held in Scetis, the Fathers treated Moses with contempt in order to test him, saying, "Why does this black man, Moses, come among us?" When he heard this, he kept silence. When the council was dismissed, they said to him, "Abba, did that not grieve you at all?" He said to them, "I was grieved, but I kept silence."

29. Abba Joseph said to Abba Nisterus, "What should I do about my tongue, for I cannot control it?" The old man said to him, "When you speak, do you find peace?" He replied, "No." The old man said, "If you do not

find peace, why do you speak? Be silent and when a conversation takes place, it is better to listen than to speak."

30. Abba Poeman also said, "A man may seem to be silent, but if his heart is condemning others he is babbling ceaselessly. But there may be another who talks from morning till night and yet he is truly silent; that is, he says nothing that is not profitable."

31. He also said, "The victory over all the afflictions that befall you, is, to keep silence."

32. He also said, "If man remembered that it is written: 'By your words you will be justified and by your words you will be condemned' (Matt. 12:37), he would choose to remain silent."

33. A brother said to Abba Poemen, "If I see something, do you want me to tell you about it?" The old man said to him, "It is written: 'If one gives answer before he hears, it is his folly and shame' (Prv. 18:13). If you are questioned, speak; if not, remain silent."

34. The old man said that a brother asked Abba Pambo if it is good to praise one's neighbor and that the old man said to him, "It is better to be silent."

35. Abba Poemen said that a brother who lived with some other brothers asked Abba Bessarion, "What ought I to do?" The old man said to him, "Keep silence and do not always be comparing yourself with others."

36. Abba Sisoes said, "If you are silent, you will have peace wherever you live."

37. A brother asked Abba Poemen, "Is it better to speak or to be silent?" The old man said to him, "The man who speaks for God's sake does well; but he who is silent for God's sake also does well."

38. Abba Poemen said, "In Abba Pambo we see three bodily activities; abstinence from food until the evening every day, silence, and much manual work."

39. It was said of Abba Poemen that if some old men were sitting with him, speaking of the ancients, and Abba Sisoes was mentioned, he would say, "Keep silence about Abba Sisoes, for that which concerns him goes beyond what can be said."

40. A brother asked Abba Sisoes, "What am I to do?"" He said to him, "What you need is a great deal of silence and humility. For it is written: 'Blessed are those who wait for him' (Is. 30:18) for thus they are able to stand."

41. Some brothers who had some seculars with them, went to see Abba Felix and they begged him to say a word to them. But the old man kept silence. After they had asked for a long time he said to them, "You wish to hear a word?" They said, "Yes, abba." Then the old man said to them, "There are no more words nowadays. When the brothers used to consult the old men and when they did what was said to them, God showed them how to speak. But now, since they ask without doing that which they hear, God has withdrawn the grace of the word from the old men and they do not find anything to say, because there are no longer any who carry their words out." Hearing this, the brothers groaned, saying, "Pray for us, abba."

42. Abba Psenthaisius, Abba Surus, and Abba Psoius used to agree in saying this, "Whenever we listened to the words of our Father, Abba Pachomius, we were greatly helped and spurred on with zeal for good works; we saw how, even when he kept silence, he taught us by his actions."[1]

NOTE

1. Online editions Apophthegmata Patrum Aegyptorium, Bousset, W., 1923; J. Chyryssavgis, K. Ware, and B. Ward, *The Spirituality of the Desert Fathers and Mothers* (Bloomington, IN: World Wisdom, 2008); G. Flood, *The Ascetic Self* (Cambridge: Cambridge University Press, 2004); D. Burton-Christie, *The Word in the Desert* (Oxfordshire: Oxford University Press, 1993); C. Barlow, *Fathers of the Church* (Washington, DC: Catholic University Press, 1969); H. Waddell, *Vitae Patrum The Desert Fathers* (London: Constable & Co., 1936); B. Ward, *The Sayings of the Desert Fathers* (Kalamazoo, MI: Cistercian Pub., 1975); J. Wortley, *The Anonymous Sayings of the Desert Fathers* (Cambridge: Cambridge University Press, 2013); C. Vaultners-Paintner, *Desert Mothers and Fathers* (Nashville, TN: Skylight Paths Pub., 2012); L. Swan, *The Forgotten Desert Mothers: Sayings, Lives, Stories* (New York: Paulist Press, 2001); D. Chitty, *The Letters of St. Antony the Great* (Oxford: SLG Press, 1975).

Chapter 6

Silence, Listening, and Benedictine Spirituality

Be silent O' heartstrings that a new melody may play in me—*Eleusinian Mysteries Hymn*[1]

SILENCE AND LISTENING

St. Benedict was a 6th-century mystic and is considered as the Father of Western Monasticism. The order of St. Benedict began in Subiaco, Italy in 529 A.D. In many ways, *The Rule of St. Benedict* can be seen as an indirect consequence of the tradition of the Desert Fathers which occurred a few centuries earlier. Benedictine spirituality began at the abbey at Monte Cassino and spread out to Italy and from there to the world. The Rule integrated prayer, manual labor, and study into a daily routine of life. Although Benedictines do not take a vow of silence, hours of strict silence are set, and at other times silence is maintained as much as is practically possible. Social conversations tend to be limited to communal recreation times.

Listening, obedience, silence, and humility each play a key role in the *Rule of St. Benedict*. From the outset, Saint Benedict makes it clear that he grounds his understanding of silence first and foremost in Scripture, particularly in the Wisdom Books of the Bible. Therefore, any form of monastic silence cannot be discussed apart from a biblical understanding of the necessity of silence in one's life; particularly one's prayer life. Silence and the Bible was discussed in an earlier chapter of this book.

So, let us now look at the *Rule of St. Benedict* concerning silence which he considers an important virtue in the Rule. Silence is mentioned in various sections of the Rule. However, of the seventy-three Sections which make up

43

the Rule, Sections 6 and 42 are the only two dedicated solely to the virtue of Silence. Here is what the Rule has to say about the virtue of Silence in Section 6:

> Let us do what the prophet says: "I will take heed of my ways, so that I do not sin with my tongue. I have watched my mouth, dumb and humbled, and kept silent even from good things" (Ps. 38:2–3). If we ought sometimes to refrain from useful speech for the sake of silence, how much more should we to abstain from evil words because of the punishment due to sin? So, considering the importance of silence, permission to speak should be seldom given to perfect disciples, even for good and holy conversation, for it is written: "If you talk a lot, you shall not escape sin," [Prov. 10:19] and "Death and life are in the power of the tongue" [Prov. 18:21]. The master may speak and teach, the disciple should be silent to listen. (*Rule of St. Benedict Sec. 6*)

This section of the Rule makes it very clear that Saint Benedict values silence and hates the sins of the tongue, especially loose words, empty chatter, or buffoonery. But the goodness and value of silence from St. Benedict's perspective far outweighs the evil he envisions in the sins of the tongue.

In Section 42, Benedict praises the cultivation of silence at all times, but especially following Night Prayer. Here is what parts of that section of the Rule have to say concerning silence:

> Monks should diligently cultivate silence at all times, but especially at night. Accordingly, this will always be the arrangement whether for fast days or for ordinary days. When there are two meals, all the monks will sit together immediately after rising from supper. Someone should read from the *Conferences* or the *Lives of the Fathers*. When all have assembled, they should pray Compline; and on leaving Compline, no one will be permitted to speak further. If anyone is found to transgress this rule of silence, he must be subjected to severe punishment, except on occasions when guests require attention or the abbot wishes to give someone a command, but even this is to be done with the utmost seriousness and proper restraint. (*Rule of St. Benedict Sec. 42*)

Obsculta! is the first instruction given by St. Benedict in his Rule. It is a Latin word which translates to our English word "listen." This word is a key for anyone who wishes to practice *the Rule of St. Benedict* and this word instructs us particularly in ways that relate primarily to the spiritual life. The type of listening the Rule implies is not simply listening with one's ears, but with the inner ear of the heart or one's entire being wholistically. The first instruction then is that Saint Benedict requires the monk to listen. But the type of listening St. Benedict imagined included a requirement that the monk should cultivate silence, humility, and obedience. These three attitudes are necessary for listening, because first of all, only the humble man listens while the prideful or self-centered man most likely believes he already knows everything there is to know. Secondly, listening requires both exterior and interior silence to enable one to hear with the ears of the heart. Third, obedience treats listening as true hearing which involves a subsequent path of potentially being a contemplative in action. The implication here is that one is not merely listening to some idle words.

All of reality is constituted with meaning. Listening in this way can enable the Holy Spirit to empower us to not only hear words spoken or written, but to reflect on them, contemplate them in silence, discern their meaning or realize their import. Ultimately, one can act on them, respond to them, or just simply be silent. Any response of silence in this fashion could be considered as active contemplation and not simply passive quietude.

Every day listening might involve not simply praying quietly and in silence, but what we might see, hear, touch, or sense in the course of our day. Listening requires our willingness to submit to demands outside of the self and a relinquishing of our self-centered preoccupations. Without doing this we cannot take on a necessary Christlikeness or a giving of ourselves to others. Because God is not only present in us, but in others in the world as well as in all of creation, we must listen not just for ourselves and our own benefit but listen to others and selflessly for others.

Much of what we experience in our daily lives or receive through our sensory perception can often get consciously overlooked by us. On several occasions while driving in our car my wife, Terri, has said to me: "Wow, look at those puffy clouds this morning." Or I might have said to her: "Look how beautiful that bougainvillea vine is in full bloom" as we walk by. We had initially perceived both the clouds and the bougainvillea somewhere in our subconscious, only in each instance we really didn't see or experience them as much as we should have or consciously wanted. It has proven to both of us that much of what each of us is experiencing daily, we are not sensing as consciously as we should until we have listened to the other's words and then truly reflected on and realized their meaning and import. In reality, God speaks through everyone and everything. Therefore, listening with our whole and entire being can create for us a greater experience of God speaking in the silence of our hearts and through the who, what, where, when, why, and how of our daily lives.

It has always been a revelation to me to realize that the word "listen" and the word "silent" contain exactly the same alphabetic letters in a different order of sequence. Surely, this might be a simple coincidence, but nonetheless I find it intriguing as it is difficult if not impossible to listen with the inner ear of the heart if one does not enter into a period of silence first. The silence at the center of one's being where God can speak to us in prayer can lead to listening to what the Lord might be saying to us throughout the day with the inner ear of our heart. Ultimately, God is our master, and as his sheep, we must be listening for the voice of the shepherd. If we are truly listening, the Lord can speak to us not only in the silence of our own interior prayer life, but through contemplation of his word in Scripture, through his real presence in the Eucharist, through the natural created world and the order of things, through his presence in our life's work, and his presence in and through others with whom we come in contact in the course of our daily routine. The Catholic Catechism refers to this simply as "Silent Love (*CC* #2717)." The Lord is silently present to us in all of these aforementioned ways. Many of these ways could be considered as "prayerful work" or "contemplation in action." St. Thomas Aquinas described prayer as "a loving awareness of God's presence." These descriptions all point to a knowledge of God's presence that is not rational or intellectual, but intuitive or a kind of "heart knowledge."[2]

Any contemplation, work, study, sacramental celebration, or reflection on the presence of God should be balanced daily with just simply taking the time to go to our inner room and pray with God in silence. Before she would enter into a time of dedicated prayer each day, Saint Elizabeth of the Trinity would offer this brief beginning prayer to God:

> O loving Incarnate Word who once, with one movement of your hand, silenced the winds and calmed the waves on Lake Gennesaret, deign to repeat this action in my soul, so that a great calm, a great silence will reign in it. O Eternal Word, utterance of my God! I long to spend my life in listening to You.[3]

St. Benedict died in 547 A.D. at Monte Cassino in Italy. Following St. Benedict's death, the number of monasteries multiplied substantially and became the primary places of silent prayer and contemplation, learning, literature, and education throughout the Western world. Throughout the centuries which followed, there had been several periods of growth and decline followed by revivification. Several reforms to this type of monastic spirituality began in the 15th century, spread throughout the Western world, and continued up into modern times.

Today, Benedictine spirituality is not only practiced by abbots or monks within the confines of any abbey but has spread out to many who consider themselves the spiritual descendants of St. Benedict and practice his Rule in the wider world. These modern-day descendants of Saint Benedict and the adherents who in many ways still practice the spirituality that has flowed out from his original Rule, have come to know the value of simply being present to the Lord in silence. Following this, they have subsequently learned how to truly listen with the core of one's being. *Obsculta!*[4]

NOTES

1. *Hymn of the Greek Mysteries*, Eleusinian Mysteries, https://www.britannica.com/topic/Eleusinian-Mysteries.

2. Ibid, Ch. 2, f. 1 (*CC* #2717); Ibid, Ch. 2, f. 3., "prayer," T. Aquinas, *Summa, Q.83, New Advent Catholic Encyclopedia*, https://www.newadvent.org/summa/3083.htm.

3. Elizabeth of the Trinity, *Elevation to the Most Holy Trinity*, https://www.carmelitedcj.org/carmel/saints-of-carmel/160-bl-elizabeth-of-the-trinity.

4. W. K. Lowther, *The Rule of St. Benedict*, translated into English (London: Pax Books, 1931). See also *The Rule of St. Benedict*, https://www.gutenberg.org/files/50040/50040-h/50040-h.htm.

Chapter 7

Eucharistic Adoration

In the Eucharist, the victory and triumph of Jesus' death are once again made present.[1]

Silence in the presence of the Holy Eucharist as loving adoration is our best initial approach because first and foremost, the Eucharist is a profound mystery that cannot be explained fully in words. Adoration itself is a human act offered to God to acknowledge His infinite character, supreme perfection, omniscience, and of our dependence upon Him for our very creation as well as our being forgiven. Although fundamentally different, the adoration we show to the infinite Lord should extend to the reverence and love we should show to any finite person created by God, because they possess inherently a sacred character. The worship of Jesus Christ as the Son of God, and given to Him as God, is designated by the Greek name *latreia*, for which the best translation in the English language we have is the word "adoration." Adoration differs from other acts of worship in that it formally consists of our self-abasement before the one true infinite God in devout recognition of His transcendent excellence and real presence among us. Our call to express the worship of the Lord in spirit and truth by our silent adoration of Him has been reaffirmed in the words of Christ in the Gospels: "The Lord your God you shall adore, and Him only shall you serve" (Mt. 4:10).

At the Last Supper, Christ had instituted the wonderful Sacrament of the Eucharist for His worshippers and adorers of all time. Here He makes Himself present to us in memory of His sacrifice on the cross and the glory of His resurrection which became the center of all history. As the Sacrament of God, Jesus has instituted this sacramental mystery of the Eucharist and entrusted it to the church. Christ has told us: "Do this in memory of me" (Lk. 22:19).

Therefore, the Eucharist can be defined as Jesus Christ's gift of Himself to us and the gift of ourselves back to Him. In the celebration of the Eucharist, all time and space has subsequently become filled with Christ. This implies that in the oneness of our lives in Christ, any moment in time and space for us can thus become a moment of Eucharistic Adoration. Because Jesus Christ is eternally present, placing ourselves in the presence of God in His Eucharist enables us to listen and allow Him to speak to us in God's language, which is Holy Silence.

This silent adoration of Jesus Christ present in the Eucharist grew out of the teaching of the Gospel writers and St. Paul. They made it plain to the Apostolic Church that the Eucharistic elements were literally Jesus Christ continuing His saving mission among men. Later in the Middle Ages, the Council of Trent would declare that Christ should be worshipped and adored now in the Eucharist no less than He had been in first century Palestine because: "In the Eucharist, it is the same God Whom the apostles adored in Galilee."[2] The silent adoration of the Eucharist has since become a longstanding article of Catholic faith.

Jesus Christ dwells in the Eucharist today just as surely as He dwelt in the village of Nazareth long ago. In mystical communion, He makes Himself present and accessible in each heart which knows Him interiorly and desires to know Him more perfectly. In the Eucharist, God's silence is the deepest as we are alone with the Lord and can allow Him to speak to our heart center where in loving tenderness, deep can speak to deep. Just like Peter, John, and James on the mountain at the transfiguration, we fall silent in faith-filled adoration gazing at Jesus alone.

At Vatican II in 1965, several of the Church's documents praised the adoration of the real presence of Christ in the Eucharist. *The Mystery of Faith*, for example, extensively treats real presence and opens with a glowing tribute to the Council's *Constitution on the Liturgy* as it praises those who: "Seek to investigate more profoundly and to understand more fruitfully the doctrine on the Holy Eucharist." Another one of the documents put forth by the Council Fathers on this was *Instruction on Eucharistic Worship*. This document was introduced with the following statement of faith: "The mystery of the Eucharist is the true center of the sacred liturgy and indeed of the whole Christian life. Consequently, the Church, guided by the Holy Spirit, continually seeks to understand and to live the Eucharist more fully."[3]

So, Eucharistic Adoration is a sign of silent devotion to and worship of Jesus Christ, who is believed by Catholics to be really present, body, blood, soul, and divinity, under the appearance of the consecrated host, that is, sacramental bread. This silent adoration is based on the tenet of the real presence of Christ in the Blessed Sacrament. Catholic doctrine holds that at the moment of consecration, the elements of bread and wine are changed (substantially) into the body, blood, soul, and divinity of Christ while the appearances (the "species") of the elements remain. In the doctrine of real presence, at the point of consecration, the act that takes place is a double miracle: 1) that Christ is present in a physical form, and 2) that the bread and wine have truly, substantially become Jesus' body and blood. Because Roman Catholics believe that Christ is truly present (body, blood, soul, and divinity) in the Eucharist, the reserved sacrament serves as a focal point of silent adoration.[4]

The word "Eucharist" can be seen as both a noun and a verb. In my personal experience of encountering the real presence of Christ in the Eucharist, I have often realized that experience more completely when I've envisioned the Eucharist as a verb, in the action and not only the object. It is true, of course, that the bread and wine really become the body and blood of Christ, but Christ is also present in the "eating of the bread" and the "drinking of the wine." Furthermore, Christ is really present in His "gifting" and our "receiving" of His body and blood. During Eucharistic Adoration, Christ is present, but also manifest in His "transforming" as well as in our "adoring." It is a matter of our experiencing real presence both in adoring through the Eucharistic action (verb) as well as the object of the Eucharist (noun).

During Eucharistic Adoration, the Eucharist oftentimes can be exposed but most often is not exposed. A lit candle will show the presence of the Blessed Sacrament in the tabernacle. The adoration in spirit can be described as an act of spiritual communion with the Lord Jesus Christ. When one enters into silent Eucharistic Adoration individually for an uninterrupted hour, this is known as a Holy Hour. The inspiration for the Holy Hour is Jesus' request of Peter in the Garden of Gethsemane the night before his crucifixion: "So, could you not keep watch with me for one hour?" (Mt. 26:40). The practice of a "Holy Hour" of silent adoration has been encouraged in the Western Catholic tradition. Mother Teresa of Calcutta had a Holy Hour each day and all members of her Missionaries of Charity followed her example. My wife Terri and I recently spent a Holy Hour in silent adoration at our local parish. The hour went by so very quickly and when we walked out of the church, we both were remarking on our Eucharistic experience of the real presence of Christ and our sensing the love of God there present with us.

In his book *The Power of Silence*, Robert Cardinal Serah has this to say about silence, adoration, and love:

> Humanity advances toward love through adoration. Sacred silence, laden with the adored presence, opens the way to mystical silence, full of loving intimacy.[5]

Hopefully, what any of us might take away from our time spent in Eucharistic Adoration is an experience of the real presence of Christ in the Holy Silence. This experience could then oftentimes manifest itself to the world as our attempts to demonstrably express our love of God and neighbor. For any of us, our adoring needs to move out from the time we spend experiencing God's presence in Eucharistic Adoration in the church to experiencing and adoring God's presence in our neighbor and in the wider world around us. God is everywhere, in everyone and everything, and always present. Silent Eucharistic Adoration needn't be restricted to our time spent adoring the Lord in a church building.

What does it mean to be silently praying before the Lord, present in the Eucharist as the Bread of Life? Our hunger for material food in some ways can be compared to the hunger in our heart and soul for the Lord. We can use the occasion of Eucharistic Adoration to truly reflect on what it means to: "Work for the food that endures to eternal life" (Jn. 6:27). Silent adoration can make the next time that we are able to receive the Eucharist at Mass as both physical and spiritual food all the more meaningful. We humans will always hunger. Jesus shows us that our hunger is not just for any material food, but for God. When he feeds us with the bread and wine of the Eucharist, he feeds our bodies with his body and nourishes our souls with his divinity. In encouraging our participation in Eucharistic Adoration, the Holy Father Pope Francis has told us:

> Immersing oneself in silent Eucharistic Adoration is the secret to knowing the Lord. . . . One cannot know the Lord without being in the habit of adoring, of adoring in silence. . . . To waste time—if I may say it—before the Lord—before the mystery of Jesus Christ. To adore, there in the silence, in the silence of adoration. He is the Lord, and I adore Him.[6]

Our silence before the Lord can induce adoration as a form not only of worship, but deep love, awe, and reverence. Since friends who love each other visit regularly, any visit to the Blessed Sacrament for the practice of silent adoration is sometimes referred to as "the practice of loving Jesus Christ." As we kneel or sit in silent adoration before this piece of bread, Christians gaze at the face of God present. In some ways, this can be compared to spouses who might gaze into each other's faces in loving adoration. The reality needs no words and is a silent spiritual embrace. After a time, the practice of Eucharistic Adoration might even allow us to not only gaze into the face of God present, but also to see the face of God in the face of our spouse, the face of a friend, a neighbor—or perhaps even a complete stranger.

Eucharistic Adoration is not simply a private alternative of what ought to be a deeply communal celebration. Rather it ought to lead those who encounter it back to the heart of that communal Eucharistic mystery where we celebrate together the Christ who is Emmanuel, that is, "God with us." Therefore, before the real presence of Christ in the Eucharist, I must continue to attempt to recognize my sinfulness, empty myself of all pride and self-seeking ambition, and allow myself to be filled with only the joy of simple silent adoration.

Finally, in the words of St. Augustine, regarding the practice of Eucharistic Adoration: "No one eats that flesh without first adoring it."[7]

NOTES

1. Ibid, Ch. 2, f. 2 (*Constitution on the Sacred Liturgy*, Vat. II, 1963).

2. Council of Trent Documents, (Trent, *Decree on the Holy Eucharist*, Ch. 5)," https://www.papalencyclicals.net/councils/trent.htm.

3. Ibid, Ch. 2, f. 2 (*Mystery of Faith, Constitution on the Liturgy, Instruction on Eucharistic Worship*, Vat II, 1963–1965).

4. Ibid, Ch. 2, f. 1 (*CC* #1330), see also https://www.usccb.org/eucharist.

5. Cardinal R. Serah, *Power of Silence* (New York: Ignatius Press, 2017), p. 122.

6. Pope Francis, *Homily Vatican City*, see https://aleteia.org/2016/10/20/eucharistic -adoration.

7. St. Augustine, *Enarrationes in Psalmos* 98, 9; see also http://communion -on-the-tongue.org/quotations.html and Pope Pius XII, *Mediator Dei*, 130, 1947, https://adoremus.org/2009/10/selections-from-papal-teaching-on-adoration-and-the -eucharist/.

Chapter 8

Silent Contemplation
of the Rosary

The Rosary can be described principally as Scripture based prayer which can be prayed audibly or in the silence of contemplative prayer. For example, the Apostles' Creed flows from our belief in the Trinity as one God in three persons which can be found in Matthew, Luke, and John's Gospel (Mt. 28:19; Lk. 3:22; Jn. 14:26). The "Our Father" or "The Lord's Prayer" can be found in both Matthew 6:9–13 and Luke 11:2–4. "The Hail Mary Prayer" can be traced to the words from the beginning of Luke's Gospel, chapter 1:28–43.[1] The various Sacred Mysteries are each drawn from the events in the life, death, resurrection, and ascension of Christ or the role of Mary, the Mother of God, in both the Scriptures and the Tradition of the church. Where these Sacred Mysteries can be found in the Bible are outlined below and are useful for silent contemplation while praying the Rosary.

Additionally, the repetitive words of the Rosary enable us to enter first into the quietude of our heart-center where the Holy Spirit dwells with us along with the repetitions of our heartbeats and unconscious breathing. The Holy Spirit present in us as well as in the Word of God in the Bible can then lead us into the silent contemplation which enables us to focus on the meditation of the scriptural verses related to the prayers and each of the various Sacred Mysteries. Each of the five events relating to the four various mysteries, Joyful, Sorrowful, Glorious, and Luminous, can be grounded primarily in the Canonical Gospels of the Bible or occasionally in the rich tradition of the church. As each mystery is entered into with each of the five decades, it is suggested that we silently reflect on each of the Bible verses pertaining to that particular event and related to that Sacred Mystery. Here is what the Catholic Catechism has to say regarding the contemplation of the Sacred Mysteries found in praying the Rosary:

Contemplative prayer is silence, the "symbol of the world to come" or "silent love." Words in this kind of prayer are not speeches; they are the kindling that feeds the fire of love. In this silence, unbearable to the "outer" man, the Father speaks to us His Incarnate Word, who suffered, died, and rose; in this silence, the spirit of adoption enables us to share in the prayer of Jesus. (*CC* #2717)[2]

THE JOYFUL MYSTERIES

The Joyful Mysteries focus on the joy which is one of the fruit of the Spirit (Gal. 5:22) flowing from God's love, given unconditionally. This joy is indeed a blessing which only comes to us through the grace of God. We can recall, intertwine, and relate any joy we have experienced in our own lives when silently contemplating the immense joy outlined in the following biblical verses.

The Annunciation (Lk. 1:26–28)

In the sixth month, the angel Gabriel was sent from God to a town of Galilee called Nazareth, to a virgin betrothed to a man named Joseph, of the house of David, and the virgin's name was Mary. And coming to her, he said, "Hail, favored one! The Lord is with you."

The Visitation (Lk. 1:39–42)

During those days Mary set out and traveled to the hill country in haste to a town of Judah, where she entered the house of Zechariah and greeted Elizabeth. When Elizabeth heard Mary's greeting, the infant leaped in her womb, and Elizabeth, filled with the Holy Spirit, cried out in a loud voice and said, "Most blessed are you among women, and blessed is the fruit of your womb."

The Nativity (Lk. 2:1–7)

In those days, a decree went out from Caesar Augustus that the whole world should be enrolled. This was the first enrollment, when Quirinius was governor of Syria. So, all went to be enrolled, each to his own town. And Joseph too went up from Galilee from the town of Nazareth to Judea, to the city of David that is called Bethlehem, because he was of the house and family of David, to be enrolled with Mary, his betrothed, who was with child. While they were there, the time came for her to have her child, and she gave birth to her firstborn son. She wrapped him in swaddling clothes and laid him in a manger, because there was no room for them in the inn.

Presentation in the Temple (Lk. 2:21–24)

When the days were completed for their purification according to the law of Moses, they took him up to Jerusalem to present him to the Lord, just as it is written in the law of the Lord, "Every male that opens the womb shall be consecrated to the Lord," and to offer the sacrifice of "a pair of turtledoves or two young pigeons," in accordance with the dictate in the law of the Lord.

Finding in the Temple (Lk. 2:41–47)

Each year his parents went to Jerusalem for the feast of Passover, and when he was twelve years old, they went up according to festival custom. After they had completed its days, as they were returning, the boy Jesus remained behind in Jerusalem, but his parents did not know it. Thinking that he was in the caravan, they journeyed for a day and looked for him among their relatives and acquaintances, but not finding him, they returned to Jerusalem to look for him. After three days they found him in the temple, sitting in the midst of the teachers, listening to them and asking them questions, and all who heard him were astounded at his understanding and his answers.

THE SORROWFUL MYSTERIES

The Sorrowful Mysteries help us to overcome any thoughts that suffering is something random in our lives. They affirm for us the fact that suffering is not something useless or outside of the circle of the divine providence of God. These mysteries help us to see that any and all suffering is wrapped up in the suffering experienced by God. We can learn the purpose of suffering in our own lives by silently contemplating the suffering outlined in those biblical verses which relate to us the suffering of Christ.

The Agony in the Garden (Mt. 26:36–39)

Then Jesus came with them to a place called Gethsemane, and he said to his disciples, "Sit here while I go over there and pray." He took along Peter and the two sons of Zebedee and began to feel sorrow and distress. Then he said to them, "My soul is sorrowful even to death. Remain here and keep watch with me." He advanced a little and fell prostrate in prayer, saying, "My Father, if it is possible, let this cup pass from me; yet, not as I will, but as you will."

Scourging at the Pillar (Mt. 27:26)

Then he released Barabbas to them, but after he had Jesus scourged, he handed him over to be crucified.

Crowning with Thorns (Mt. 27:27–29)

Then the soldiers of the governor took Jesus inside the praetorium and gathered the whole cohort around him. They stripped off his clothes and threw a scarlet military cloak about him. Weaving a crown out of thorns, they placed it on his head, and a reed in his right hand. And kneeling before him, they mocked him, saying, "Hail, King of the Jews!"

Carrying the Cross (Mk. 15:21–22)

They pressed into service a passer-by, Simon, a Cyrenian, who was coming in from the country, the father of Alexander and Rufus, to carry his cross. They brought him to the place of Golgotha (which is translated Place of the Skull).

Crucifixion and Death (Lk. 23:33–46)

When they came to the place called the Skull, they crucified him and the criminals there, one on his right, the other on his left. [Then Jesus said, "Father, forgive them, they know not what they do."] They divided his garments by casting lots. The people stood by and watched; the rulers, meanwhile, sneered at him and said, "He saved others, let him save himself if he is the chosen one, the Messiah of God." Even the soldiers jeered at him. As they approached to offer him wine. They called out, "If you are King of the Jews, save yourself." Above him there was an inscription that read, "This is the King of the Jews." Now one of the criminals hanging there reviled Jesus, saying, "Are you not the Messiah? Save yourself and us." The other, however, rebuking him, said in reply, "Have you no fear of God, for you are subject to the same condemnation? And indeed, we have been condemned justly, for the sentence we received corresponds to our crimes, but this man has done nothing criminal." Then he said, "Jesus, remember me when you come into your kingdom." He replied to him, "Amen, I say to you, today you will be with me in Paradise." It was now about noon and darkness came over the whole land until three in the afternoon because of an eclipse of the sun. Then the veil of the temple was torn down the middle. Jesus cried out in a loud voice, "Father, into your hands I commend my spirit"; and when he had said this he breathed his last.

THE GLORIOUS MYSTERIES

The Glorious Mysteries focus on the fact that the faith, hope, and love in our lives is all tied to the resurrection of Christ from the dead. As the Apostle Paul told us: "If Christ is not raised our faith is useless." The "rising" which relates to our own lives can only come to us because death has been defeated by Jesus Christ. As we silently contemplate the following Biblical verses, we can give thanks, praise, and all glory to God that there might be more to our own lives than just the earthly life we are currently living and the eventual earthly horizon that will bring about our own death prior to rising.

The Resurrection (Lk. 24:1–6)

But at daybreak on the first day of the week they took the spices they had prepared and went to the tomb. They found the stone rolled away from the tomb; but when they entered, they did not find the body of the Lord Jesus. While they were puzzling over this, behold, two men in dazzling garments appeared to them. They were terrified and bowed their faces to the ground. They said to them, "Why do you seek the living one among the dead? He is not here, but he has been raised."

The Ascension (Mk. 16:19)

So, then the Lord Jesus, after he spoke to them, was taken up into heaven and took his seat at the right hand of God.

Descent of the Holy Spirit (Acts 2:1–4)

When the time for Pentecost was fulfilled, they were all in one place together. And suddenly there came from the sky a noise like a strong driving wind, and it filled the entire house in which they were. Then there appeared to them tongues as of fire, which parted and came to rest on each one of them. And they were all filled with the Holy Spirit and began to speak in different tongues, as the Spirit enabled them to proclaim.

The Assumption of Mary (Lk. 1:48–49)

For he has looked upon his handmaid's lowliness; behold, from now on will all ages call me blessed. The Mighty One has done great things for me, and holy is his name.

Coronation of Mary (Rev. 12:1)

A great sign appeared in the sky, a woman clothed with the sun, with the moon under her feet, and on her head a crown of twelve stars.

THE LUMINOUS MYSTERIES

The Luminous Mysteries enable us to silently contemplate the following Biblical verses that essentially describe to us in part how and why Christ is the "light of the world." Reflecting on these mysteries can allow us to come to know Jesus better. Any enlightenment we might experience in our own lives comes to us through the light of Christ in the power of the Holy Spirit. This can occur because the Holy Spirit is present in us and in the Word of God. If we are open and welcome the grace of God, the light of Christ will lift our blindness and radiantly shine on all the dark corners of our lives.

Baptism of Christ (Mt. 3:16–17)

After Jesus was baptized, he came up from the water and behold, the heavens were opened [for him], and he saw the Spirit of God descending like a dove [and] coming upon him. And a voice came from the heavens, saying, "This is my beloved Son, with whom I am well pleased."

Wedding Feast at Cana (Jn. 2:1–5)

On the third day there was a wedding in Cana in Galilee, and the mother of Jesus was there. Jesus and his disciples were also invited to the wedding. When the wine ran short, the mother of Jesus said to him, "They have no wine." [And] Jesus said to her, "Woman, how does your concern affect me? My hour has not yet come." His mother said to the servers, "Do whatever he tells you."

Proclaiming the Kingdom (Mk. 1:14–15)

After John had been arrested, Jesus came to Galilee proclaiming the gospel of God: "This is the time of fulfillment. The kingdom of God is at hand. Repent, and believe in the gospel."

The Transfiguration (Mt. 17:1–2)

After six days Jesus took Peter, James, and John his brother, and led them up a high mountain by themselves. And he was transfigured before them; his face shone like the sun and his clothes became white as light.

Institution of the Eucharist (Mt. 26:26–29)

While they were eating, Jesus took bread, said the blessing, broke it, and giving it to his disciples said, "Take and eat; this is my body." Then he took a cup, gave thanks, and gave it to them, saying, "Drink from it, all of you, for this is my blood of the covenant, which will be shed on behalf of many for the forgiveness of sins. I tell you, from now on I shall not drink this fruit of the vine until the day when I drink it with you new in the kingdom of my Father."

ROSARY BEADS

In praying the Rosary, a counting apparatus is often used such as Rosary beads. This practice was said to have begun among the early monks and ascetics of the desert who used pebbles on a string or tied knots in a rope to count the prayers in silence. The name "Rosary" comes from *Rosarius*, which is Latin for "A garland of roses" and is a metaphorical description of the practice. The word "bead" comes from an old Anglo-Saxon word *bede*, which simply means "prayer." The fingering of the beads tied to repetitive prayer can sometimes release a calming spiritual energy sent by the Holy Spirit to our heart-center. This can help to make us receptive to the all-encompassing silence in contemplating the Sacred Mysteries as well as tranquil and peaceful with the repetition of the prayers. It also serves to rid us of any unnecessary worries, fears, and anxieties. Because of this, one could make a comparison here to the practice of centering prayer. So, saying the Rosary is not as simplistic as reciting fifty Hail Mary's and a few Our Father's. That type of thinking misses the purpose of the Rosary and the immense richness found in silent contemplation of the Sacred Mysteries. Pope John Paul II has told us in his *Apostolic Letter on the Holy Rosary*: "Without the Rosary's contemplative dimension, it would lose its meaning. Without contemplation, the Rosary is a body without a soul."[3]

And yet some might still ask, "Why do we repetitively say all those Hail Mary's?" St. Louis de Montfort has said, "It would be easier to separate light from the sun than Mary from Jesus."[4] Therefore, no divine person is independent of another. The Word of God incorporates the plan of God. It is an economy of salvation. Our faith is unified and not a diversity of unrelated truths or unrelated divine persons. Mary, as the Mother of God, has intrinsic value in the incarnation of Jesus Christ, her Son and God's Son. After we say all those repetitive Hail Mary prayers and then silently ponder the various Sacred Mysteries about Mary or which include Mary, we can visualize and reflect on God's loving action in her. We can then relate that to God's loving action in our own lives. During the reading of the Sacred Mysteries from the Bible, we can silently contemplate the mystery of Mary's simple faith, her unfailing hope, and unconditional love, as well as her virtues, and complete trust in God's Word. Any Christian who has prayed the Rosary repetitively, like a child calling for its mother, shall claim the Mother of God as their intercessor when they stand before the throne of God. Having prayed in the "Hail Mary" over and over: "Pray for us sinners now and at the hour of our death."

Could they expect anything less? Finally, we can go to Jesus through Mary, God's Mother and ours. She is an intricate part of the entire mystery of God which is meant to be contemplated by us though still mostly hidden away in Holy Silence.

NOTES

1. Ibid, Ch. 1, f. 3.
2. Ibid, Ch. 2, f. 1 (*CC* #2717).
3. John Paul II, *Apostolic Letter on the Holy Rosary*, it, Ch. 1, #12, 2002.
4. St. Louis de Montfort, *The Littlest Souls*, https://littlestsouls.wordpress.com/tag/st-louis-de-montfort/.

How to recite the Holy Rosary

1. SAY THESE PRAYERS…

IN THE NAME of the Father, and of the Son, and of the Holy Spirit. Amen. (As you say this, with your right hand touch your forehead when you say Father, touch your breastbone when you say Son, touch your left shoulder when you say Holy, and touch your right shoulder when you say Spirit.)

I BELIEVE IN GOD, the Father almighty, Creator of Heaven and earth. And in Jesus Christ, His only Son, our Lord, Who was conceived by the Holy Spirit, born of the Virgin Mary, suffered under Pontius Pilate; was crucified, died, and was buried. He descended into Hell. The third day He rose again from the dead. He ascended into Heaven, and sits at the right hand of God, the Father almighty. He shall come again to judge the living and the dead. I believe in the Holy Spirit, the holy Catholic Church, the communion of saints, the forgiveness of sins, the resurrection of the body, and life everlasting. Amen.

OUR FATHER, Who art in Heaven, hallowed be Thy Name. Thy kingdom come, Thy will be done on earth as it is in Heaven. Give us this day our daily bread, and forgive us our trespasses, as we forgive those who trespass against us. And lead us not into temptation, but deliver us from evil. Amen.

HAIL MARY, full of grace, the Lord is with thee. Blessed art thou among women, and blessed is the fruit of thy womb, Jesus. Holy Mary, Mother of God, pray for us sinners, now and at the hour of our death. Amen.

GLORY BE to the Father, and to the Son, and to the Holy Spirit. As it was in the beginning is now, and ever shall be, world without end. Amen.

O MY JESUS, forgive us our sins, save us from the fires of Hell; lead all souls to Heaven, especially those in most need of Thy mercy. Amen.

HAIL HOLY QUEEN, mother of mercy; our life, our sweetness, and our hope. To thee do we cry, poor banished children of Eve. To thee do we send up our sighs, mourning and weeping in this vale of tears. Turn, then, most gracious advocate, thine eyes of mercy toward us. And after this, our exile, show unto us the blessed fruit of thy womb, Jesus. O clement, O loving, O sweet Virgin Mary. Pray for us, O holy Mother of God, that we may be made worthy of the promises of Christ. Amen.

O GOD, WHOSE only-begotten Son by His life, death and resurrection, has purchased for us the rewards of eternal life; grant, we beseech Thee, that by meditating upon these mysteries of the Most Holy Rosary of the Blessed Virgin Mary, we may imitate what they contain and obtain what they promise, through the same Christ our Lord. Amen.

ANNOUNCE each mystery by saying something like, " The third Joyful Mystery Is the Birth of Our Lord." This is required only when saying the Rosary in a group.

2. IN THIS ORDER…

INTRODUCTION
1. IN THE NAME…
2. I BELIEVE IN GOD…
3. OUR FATHER…
4. HAIL MARY…
5. HAIL MARY…
6. HAIL MARY…
7. GLORY BE…
8. O MY JESUS…

THE FIRST DECADE
9. ANNOUNCE…
10. OUR FATHER…
11. HAIL MARY…
12. HAIL MARY…
13. HAIL MARY…
14. HAIL MARY…
15. HAIL MARY…
16. HAIL MARY…
17. HAIL MARY…
18. HAIL MARY…
19. HAIL MARY…
20. HAIL MARY…
21. GLORY BE…
22. O MY JESUS…

THE SECOND DECADE
23. ANNOUNCE
24. OUR FATHER…
25. HAIL MARY…
26. HAIL MARY…
27. HAIL MARY…
28. HAIL MARY…
29. HAIL MARY…
30. HAIL MARY…
31. HAIL MARY…
32. HAIL MARY…
33. HAIL MARY…
34. HAIL MARY…
35. GLORY BE…
36. O MY JESUS…

THE THIRD DECADE
37. ANNOUNCE…
38. OUR FATHER…
39. HAIL MARY…
40. HAIL MARY…
41. HAIL MARY…
42. HAIL MARY…
43. HAIL MARY…
44. HAIL MARY…
45. HAIL MARY…
46. HAIL MARY…
47. HAIL MARY…
48. HAIL MARY…
49. GLORY BE…
50. O MY JESUS…

THE FOURTH DECADE
51. ANNOUNCE…
52. OUR FATHER…
53. HAIL MARY…
54. HAIL MARY…
55. HAIL MARY…
56. HAIL MARY…
57. HAIL MARY…
58. HAIL MARY…
59. HAIL MARY…
60. HAIL MARY…
61. HAIL MARY…
62. HAIL MARY…
63. GLORY BE…
64. O MY JESUS…

THE FIFTH DECADE
65. ANNOUNCE…
66. OUR FATHER…
67. HAIL MARY…
68. HAIL MARY…
69. HAIL MARY…
70. HAIL MARY…
71. HAIL MARY…
72. HAIL MARY…
73. HAIL MARY…
74. HAIL MARY…
75. HAIL MARY…
76. HAIL MARY…
77. GLORY BE…
78. O MY JESUS…

CONCLUSION
79. HAIL HOLY QUEEN…
80. O GOD, WHOSE…
81. IN THE NAME…

3. WHILE TOUCHING THESE BEADS TO KEEP TRACK OF YOUR PROGRESS…

4. AND SILENTLY MEDITATING ON THESE " MYSTERIES", OR EVENTS FROM THE LIVES OF JESUS AND MARY…

On Monday and Saturday, meditate on the "Joyful Mysteries"
First Decade (Steps 9-22): The Annunciation of Gabriel to Mary (Luke 1:26-38)
Second Decade (Steps 23-36): The Visitation of Mary to Elizabeth (Luke 1:39-56)
Third Decade (Steps 37-50): The Birth of Our Lord (Luke 2:1-21)
Fourth Decade (Steps 51-64): The Presentation of Our Lord (Luke 2:22-38)
Fifth Decade (Steps 65-78): The Finding of Our Lord in the Temple (Luke 2:41-52)

On Thursday, meditate on the "Luminous Mysteries"
First Decade: The Baptism of Our Lord in the River Jordan (Matthew 3:13-16)
Second Decade: The Wedding at Cana, when Christ manifested Himself (Jn 2:1-11)
Third Decade: The Proclamation of the Kingdom of God (Mark 1:14-15)
Fourth Decade: The Transfiguration of Our Lord (Matthew 17:1-8)
Fifth Decade: The Last Supper, when Our Lord gave us the Holy Eucharist (Mt 26)

On Tuesday and Friday, meditate on the "Sorrowful Mysteries"
First Decade: The Agony of Our Lord in the Garden (Matthew 26:36-56)
Second Decade: Our Lord is Scourged at the Pillar (Matthew 27:26)
Third Decade: Our Lord is Crowned with Thorns (Matthew 27:27-31)
Fourth Decade: Our Lord Carries the Cross to Calvary (Matthew 27:32)
Fifth Decade: The Crucifixion of Our Lord (Matthew 27:33-56)

On Wednesday and Sunday, meditate on the "Glorious Mysteries"
First Decade: The Glorious Resurrection of Our Lord (John 20:1-29)
Second Decade: The Ascension of Our Lord (Luke 24:36-53)
Third Decade: The Descent of the Holy Spirit at Pentecost (Acts 2:1-41)
Fourth Decade: The Assumption of Mary into Heaven
Fifth Decade: The Coronation of Mary as Queen of Heaven and Earth

You are encouraged to copy and distribute this sheet.

www.newadvent.org

Figure 8.1. How to Recite the Holy Rosary

Chapter 9

The Silent Poor

The fruit of silence is prayer,

The fruit of prayer is faith,

The fruit of faith is love,

And the fruit of love is service.[1]

—Mother Teresa of Calcutta

THE ANAWIM

Anawim is a Hebrew word from the Old Testament which described the "poor and lowly ones" who remained faithful to God, especially during times of great difficulty. They were the humble, often silent and overlooked people who became known as the *anawim* because they were the "faithful remnant "of Yahweh. They were oppressed, persecuted, marginalized, and given no voice. Only the Lord and those who were faithful to God's covenant were the ones who were given a mandate to speak for the *anawim*. Thus, these "poor ones" showed their trust in God by being faithful to his covenant during the times they were bowed down in prayer for deliverance from oppression. The trust in God by the *anawim* was rooted from the beginning in the words of the Torah and later in the Pentateuch that Yahweh is the protector and defender of the poor and lowly. And as the people of God, followers of Yahweh were to open their hands and hearts to the poor in their midst (Ex. 22:22–25; Dt. 15:7–11).[2]

Due to their suffering in silence, lowly status, simple faith, humbleness of heart, and vulnerability, the *anawim* were the elect of Yahweh and had to depend totally on the grace, goodness, and mercy of God. As we are told later in several of the Psalms for example:

The righteous cry out, the Lord hears, and he rescues them from all their afflictions. The Lord is close to the brokenhearted and saves those whose spirit is crushed (the anawim) (Ps. 34:18–19).

Yahweh loves his people and he adorns the lowly (the anawim) with victory (Ps. 149:4).

Yahweh hears the cry of the poor (the anawim) and his own who are in bonds he spurns not (Ps. 68:3).

Later in the New Testament, we will find that Mary of Nazareth held a special place and was given a singular role among all the *anawim*. Her life was hidden in silence and was a life of quiet humility and faith-filled obedience to the Lord. This singled her out for a special place in God's salvific plan. She allowed the Holy Spirit to work in her and proclaimed in her Magnificat that the Almighty had done great things for her in her lowliness in contrast to God's dealings with the proud and lofty:

My soul proclaims the greatness of the Lord; my spirit rejoices in God my savior. For he has looked upon his handmaid's lowliness; behold, from now on will all ages call me blessed. The Mighty One has done great things for me and holy is his name. His mercy is from age to age to those who fear him. He has shown might with his arm, dispersed the arrogant of mind and heart. He has thrown down the rulers from their thrones but lifted up the lowly. The hungry he has filled with good things; the rich he has sent away empty. (Lk. 1:46–53)

Subsequently, after Mary gave birth to Jesus through the Holy Spirit, Jesus Christ will see himself as being the Savior, defender and deliverer of the *anawim* as he tells us in Luke's Gospel: "The Spirit of the Lord is upon me because he has anointed me to preach the good news to the poor. He has sent me to proclaim release to the captives and recovery of sight to the blind, to set at liberty those who are oppressed, to proclaim the acceptable year of the Lord" (Lk. 4:18–19).

In our own day and time, Pope Francis takes his place among those in the Church who take up the Old Testament Tradition and then continue Jesus' role as defender of the *anawim*, those who are the poor, oppressed, and suffering in silence. The Holy Father tells us:

In myriad ways poverty challenges us daily, in faces marked by suffering, marginalization, oppression, violence, torture and imprisonment, war, deprivation of freedom and dignity, ignorance and illiteracy, medical emergencies and shortage of work, trafficking and slavery, exile, extreme poverty and forced migration. Poverty has the face of women, men and children exploited by base interests, crushed by the machinations of power and money.[3]

In so many parts of the world there are children who have nothing to eat. That's not news, it seems normal. It cannot be this way! Yet these things become the norm: that some homeless people die of cold on the streets is not news. In contrast, a ten-point drop in the stock markets is a tragedy! A person dying is not news, but if the stock market drops ten points, it is a tragedy. Thus, people are disposed of as if they were trash.[4]

THE UNBORN

Whether called "babies" or "fetuses," in the world today, there are approximately seventy-five million unborn who are aborted each year. This equates to just under one-third of all pregnancies worldwide. According to the Guttmacher Institute and the Center for Disease Control, there are currently just under one million abortions that occur in the United States each year.[5]

The unborn are completely silent, helpless, dependent, and are totally voiceless. The only voice they have are the voices of those who are willing to speak for them. This is not to say that a woman should have no voice or that women should not speak for themselves or have those who choose to speak for them and their basic human rights. Only that, unlike most women, the unborn would be completely and totally silent without the other voices who have chosen and will choose to speak for them. They are truly the *anawim* and among the poorest of the poor. They are totally innocent, defenseless, and completely reliant on the grace of God to stir the presence of the Holy Spirit within other persons to be their voices. We entrust the lives of all those who are unborn to Mary, the Mother of God, the Mother of Jesus, and the Mother of all who are alive in Christ, born and unborn.

THE SILENCE OF THE POOR

The Lord is a good listener. That is probably why: "The Lord hears the cry of the poor" (Ps. 34). The poor are relegated to silence because very often it seems no one except the Lord is listening for that still small voice. Currently there exists a disturbing trend, whereby mass poverty has almost entirely receded from the conversation of many people in America—despite hitting its worst levels since President Lyndon B. Johnson declared a war on poverty almost five decades ago. There is a growing indifference that fosters the silence of chronic poverty because it enables some human beings to reject others who are relegated to having little or no voice. What is necessary is not only a sharing of unequal resources but also a spirituality of solidarity. This can bring to the silent poor a renewed hope for revitalization and a partial lifting of the yoke of chronic despair that they often experience.

Here is what the Vatican Council II document on the *Apostolate on the Laity* states in regard to solidarity in Christ, the plight of the silent poor, and the consolation of Christian love:

> Assuming human nature, Christ bound the whole human race to Himself as a family through a certain supernatural solidarity and established love as the mark of His disciples. Whereas there are people in need of food and drink, clothing, housing, medicine, employment, and education, wherever persons lack the facilities necessary for living a truly human life or are afflicted with serious distress, illness or suffer exile or imprisonment, there Christian love should seek them out and find them to console them.[6]

Another key document generated at Vatican II was the Pastoral Constitution on the Church (*Gaudium et Spes*). This pastoral document opens with the following statement:

> The joys and hopes, griefs and anxieties of the people of this age, especially those who are poor or in any way afflicted, those too are the joys and hopes, the griefs and anxieties of the followers of Christ.[7]

Why is it necessary for we as Christians to be in solidarity with the poorest and weakest in society? One of the primary reasons is because we must recognize that God has conferred on all human persons an inherent human dignity, and this implies that every member of society has been given basic human rights. Solidarity is a spirit of unity that bonds us together as a community of persons including and especially the poorest, weakest, and most vulnerable. It emphasizes love which the Sacred Scriptures and a long tradition of Catholic social teaching tell us is the glue that bonds us together. Jesus Christ is at the center of Christian solidarity and thus makes it more powerful and mystical than mere fellowship.

It is when the poor are ignored, overlooked, or mistreated, whether intentionally or unintentionally, that Christian solidarity demands that some persons in solidarity must speak for others who are rendered as silent and have not been given a voice. Their cries of hunger, for basic human necessities, human dignity, or the lifting of the yoke of oppression, may have largely gone unheard by society. This is sometimes referred to as creating a need for Christians in solidarity with the silent poor to then make what is termed a "preferential option for the poor."[8]

"Preferential option for the poor" is solidly rooted in both the Old and New Testament of the Bible as well as the Judeo-Christian Tradition (Ex. 22:20–26; Lv. 19:9–10; Jb. 34:20–28; Pr. 31:8–9; Is. 25:4–5, 58:5–7; Mt. 25:34–40; Lk. 4:16–21, 6: 20–23). It refers to a thread which runs throughout the entire Bible describing how preference is given by God, the prophets, and all righteous persons to the well-being of the poorest, most vulnerable, and powerless, who are the silent poor. As Christians we are called to look at the world from the perspective of those who are not only materially poor, but also all those without a voice who are the most vulnerable or marginalized. Being in solidarity with them is where Jesus was often found and because God is most often found among the poorest and powerless, we are called to be in solidarity as their Christian brothers and sisters who are essentially contemplatives in action. Jesus has promised us that He would always be in our midst until the end of time. So, the poor in many ways are a sacrament of the presence of God among us. In many ways, they become the voice of our God who speaks in silence. This also can be seen as arising in some ways from the Catholic experience of the real presence of Christ in the Eucharist. The Bible and the tradition of the Catholic church both further teach us:

In every human being, above all in the least among us, one meets Christ himself (cf. Mt. 25:40).[9]

The Eucharist commits us to the poor. To receive in truth the body and blood of Christ given up for us, we must recognize Christ in the poorest, his brethren (*CC* #137).[10]

To receive in truth the body and blood of Christ given up for us, we must recognize Christ in the poorest (*CC* #1397).[11]

If society at large does not somehow recognize a "preferential option for the poor," then by default, it makes a "preferential option for the status quo." Furthermore, it fails to understand that any social or economic question today has a worldwide dimension, and any one part of society often affects other parts of society. The resulting loss of human dignity and human rights of the poorest through silencing, oppression, marginalization, and powerlessness ends up wounding all of society. The building of walls, whether physical or spiritual to maintain inequality, denies fundamental rights and keeps some poor persons from having a voice in society and only heightens the silence of the poor. This also allows some persons to perceive others who live in extreme poverty as an outright threat to security, democracy, and peace. This fuels efforts to ensure that some societal poor are perpetually kept silent in order to maintain a false sense of security, a pseudo-democracy, and an illusional peace. This peace is unsustainable because it has no foundation of love and is lacking in justice. Where there is no love or justice there can be no peace; it becomes an illusion. In a different world ruled by love and concern for the common good of all humanity including the poorest, rather than a quest for profit, peace would become possible as the result of a more perfect justice among all persons.[12]

In reality, the silence of the poor ends up masking the percolating violence bubbling up like the inner core of a volcano beneath it. Another type of silence also covers over the normalization of the violence on the part of those of us who are not materially poor but refuse to use our voice to speak out against "a preferential option for the status quo." This is extreme violence in the sense that it seeks to silence those who are the victims of the cycles of poverty and ultimately makes them not only silent, but in addition to being voiceless, they become increasingly irrelevant and then ultimately invisible.

Pope Saint John Paul II has told us in his writings that, "The needs of the poor must be given preference to the wants and desires of the rich."[13] The silent poor are part of those three billion people in our world who are needy, nameless, and ultimately depersonalized. They are those whose cries to God have been mostly drowned out and gone unheard by those of us who live our lives in a noisy, frenzied, chaotic, and bustling world which feeds off a consumerist society. We are like hamsters on a treadmill who live in a land of opportunity we call "the American dream," but the silent poor who do not participate are forced to live a nightmarish existence. We prohibit them, whether intentionally or unintentionally, from being any kind of full societal participants or even simply "American dreamers."

Because we live with an excess and more than what we need to live, others are forced to live with almost nothing at all. They are deprived of basic human needs which are theirs by right such as sustainable food, safe drinking water, health, shelter, and education. By focusing on our wants and desires instead of our needs, we ignore their human dignity, outright deny their basic human rights, and often even their very existence. We steadfastly refuse to hear their voices and ignore their cries because we are afraid to try to understand and accept the reality of their horrifying existence. As soon as we begin to hear their voices, we may have to attempt to bring them out of their silence and into the whispers of our consciousness. This carries with it a recognition that it is we who, in some ways, have forced upon them their reality through our intended and unintended acts of social and economic violence. Their cries of intense hunger, powerlessness, hopelessness, humiliation, and unfulfilled longing are then not just heard by the Lord and those who currently share their same experience, but will also begin to be heard by more of us in society who cannot deny that we have heard that still small voice of the Lord.

Finally, it should be understood, that our response to the silent poor should not be material assistance alone. It should include efforts to make them increasingly self-reliant as full and productive participants because full participation is one of the pillars of any true democracy.[14] It should also include advocacy for social and economic reform by speaking truth to power. This includes speaking out against unjust persons, institutions, and systems of government. It is then that the voice of the silent poor will begin to be heard not only by the Lord, who always hears the cry of the poor, but by all of us who are listening with the ears of our hearts. It is in the Gospels that Jesus asks us,

> Who, then, is the faithful and prudent servant, to whom the master has put in charge of his household to distribute to them their food at the proper time? (Mt. 24:45)

NOTES

1. Online Mother Teresa of Calcutta, https://www.quoteperson.com/quoteid /1462; see also https://developingsuperleaders.wordpress.com/2021/01/25/the-fruit -of-silence-is-prayer-the-fruit-of-prayer-is-faith-the-fruit-of-faith-is-love-the-fruit-of -faith-is-love-the-fruit-of-love-is-service-the-fruit-of-service-is-peace-saint-mother-t /.

2. Ibid, Ch. 1, f. 3, Torah; see also https://www.chabad.org/library/bible_cdo/aid /63255/jewish/The-Bible-with-Rashi.htm.

3. Pope Francis, *World Day of the Poor* (Vatican Radio, June 13, 2017).

4. Pope Francis, *World Environment Day* (www.HuffingtonPost, June 5, 2013, #3390299).

5. https://www.guttmacher.org/gpr/2019/09/us-abortion-rate-continues-drop -once-again-state-abortion-restrictions-are-not-main; see also https://www.cdc.gov/ reproductivehealth/data_stats/abortion.htm.

6. Ibid, Ch. 2, f. 2, Vat. Council II (*Decree on the Apostolate of the Laity*, 1965).

7. Ibid, Ch. 2, f. 2, Vat. Council II (*Gaudium et Spes* #1, 1965).

8. Ibid, Ch. 2, f. 1 (*CC* #2444, #2448); see also https://www.usccb.org/beliefs -and-teachings/what-we-believe/catholic-social-teaching/option-for-the-poor-and -vulnerable.

9. Ibid, Ch. 1, f. 3; see also Ibid, Ch. 2, f. 2, Vat. Council II (*Dignitatis Personae*, 1965), https://www.vatican.va/roman_curia/congregations/cfaith/documents).

10. Ibid, Ch. 2, f. 1 (*CC* #137).

11. Ibid, Ch. 2, f. 1 (*CC* #1397).

12. See Pope John Paul II (*Solicitudo Rei Socialis* #10,59, 1987); see also https://www.vatican.va/content/john-paul-ii/en/encyclicals/documents/hf_jp-ii_enc _30121987_sollicitudo-rei-socialis.html.

13. Pope John Paul II (*ADDRESS OF POPE JOHN PAUL II TO THE MEMBERS OF DIFFERENT CHURCHES AND CHRISTIAN COMMUNIONS, #5*, 1984); see https://www.vatican.va/content/john-paul-ii/en/speeches/1984/september/documents/ hf_jp-ii_spe_19840914_confessioni-cristiane.html.

14. Pope Leo (*Rerum Novarum*, 1891), https://www.vatican.va/content/leo-xiii /en/encyclicals/documents/hf_l-xiii_enc_15051891_rerum-novarum.html; Pope John Paul II (*Laborem Exercen,* 1981), https://www.vatican.va/content/john-paul-ii

/en/encyclicals/documents/hf_jp-ii_enc_14091981_laborem-exercens.html; see also
Michael Hickey, *Catholic Social Teaching and Distributism: Toward a New Economy*
(Lanham, MD: Hamilton Books, 2018), pp. 23–25.

Chapter 10

Hesychasm and Centering Prayer

Silence is the language of God, all else is a poor translation.—Rumi[1]

HESYCHASM

Hesychasm is silent, still, quiet, and peaceful prayer. It is the central consideration in the prayer of the Desert Fathers whom we discuss in chapter 5. On an external level, it signifies someone living a life apart from the hustle and bustle of the world as we know it. However, on a much deeper level, it is not merely separation from chaos, noise and speaking with others, but the possession of interior silence and tranquil peace at our heart-center. Thus, it is entirely possible to use this term of many who do not actually live an ascetic life in the desert. It can mean, more specifically, an attempt to be constantly present to and with God and the possession of an interior silence which can empower us to listen more closely to what the Lord might be saying to us. "Hesychasm" is a more general term and "hesychast" is a noun sometimes used to describe any person who seeks to follow this way of silent interior prayer.

Hesychasts generally believe that one can come closer to knowing God and union with God through purity of soul and interior silent prayer than by several years of intense theological study. They would make a distinction between knowing about God and knowing God. Hesychasm, as a two-thousand-year-old practice of prayer, takes its name from the Greek root of the word which is translated as "to be silent" or "to be still." Much of what we know about it is taken from the writings of Saint John Chrysostrom, the Cappadocians, Evagarius, the sayings of the Desert Fathers, and the mystics of the Christian religion from the 4th century onward.[2]

When the Christian church split into "Catholic" and "Orthodox" in the 11th century, hesychasm disappeared from most of all from Western culture as it was recognized as being too individualistic and far less communal. It was the Orthodox church that continued to preserve the hesychastic form of the prayer of silent interior stillness. Hesychasm had been recovered by Westerners beginning in the Middle Ages. At that time, it involved a shift from self-centered or egocentric prayer to a form of transcendent or God-centered consciousness where it could then be described as union with the God of mystery who speaks in the language of Holy Silence.

In his exploration of the movement of the soul through *The Dark Night of the Soul*,[3] St. John of the Cross, the father of mystical theology, used the image of a house grown silent and still to describe how the soul can be centered in God through prayer. There it is free to leave behind the self and become absorbed in Christ. It is in this silence that God's love is found dwelling and hidden in the inner secret room of the soul. From this inner love, all outward peace and tranquility begins to flow.

There are essentially three steps required in hesychastic prayer:

1. Detachment: This involves a detachment from our words, thoughts, senses, and emotions as well as the things of the world as we know it.
2. Stillness: This involves a detachment from the intellect and imagination. One embraces stillness and silence both physically and spiritually. Detachment from all noise, chaos, and distractions is a critical element here.
3. Illumination: This final step has more to do with the grace of God who speaks to us in silence. It involves mystical union with God at our heart-center. All we can do is facilitate the path to this final step by the prior two steps in this process and then be completely open to allowing the grace of God to do the rest. To enter this state where our consciousness is transcended, some have recommended the repeated use of what is called "The Jesus Prayer."[4] This involves the repetition of the following words: "Lord Jesus have mercy on me, a sinner." These few words are not spoken audibly or outwardly, but inwardly in the silence of our hearts. Here we only consciously attempt to move our mind and mental prayer into our heart-center. It must become an unconscious prayer specifically of our hearts. This is not something that occurs as metaphysical expression, but moreover is taken quite literally. In this third stage, God sheds uncreated light, divine light, or the light of the Holy Spirit which we can only see or hear with the eyes and ears of our hearts.

In writing on hesychastic prayer, Pope St. John Paul II, has said,

This term (*hesychasm*) refers to a practice of prayer marked by deep tranquility of the spirit contemplating God unceasingly by invoking the name of Jesus. It stresses that man is offered the concrete possibility of uniting with God in his inner heart in a profound union of grace.[5]

This illumination is often identified with the movement of the Holy Spirit as divine light. The hesychastic tradition is now resurfacing within the Roman Catholic church. In many ways, the hesychastic tradition was the forerunner of what today might be called "centering prayer."

CENTERING PRAYER

Centering prayer has a long tradition in the Christian church beginning with the hesychastic prayer of the desert fathers and the Eastern Orthodox churches on down to the Benedictine monks, John of the Cross and other mystics. In this century it has been reintroduced and practiced by Thomas Merton, Fr. Thomas Keating, Fr. Basil Pennington, and many other devotees of the practice. The name, "centering prayer," was taken from Thomas Merton's description of contemplative prayer (a much older and more traditional practice) as prayer that is "centered entirely on the presence of God."[6] Merton's books on the subject, for example, *Seven Story Mountain, Contemplative Prayer*, and others,[7] helped to revive this practice of centering without words, thoughts, or images which had long been practiced in the Eastern Orthodox churches but had seemingly been forgotten in the West.

In addition to the calm quiet this practice brings to our physical body, centering involves the quieting of our mind, heart, and will so that we might listen for what God might be saying to us in silence. Centering will take us to a place beyond any words, thoughts, ideas, images, feelings, or emotions. It is a transition to the very heart-most grounding of our being to find transformation. Jesus would often slip away from the crowds to find a quiet and peaceful place to gather himself, pray and listen to what the Father was saying. Furthermore, we find the seeds of centering in the Gospels as Jesus says to his disciples:

When you pray, go to your inner room, close the door, and pray to your Father in secret. And your Father who sees in secret will repay you. In praying, do not babble like the pagans, who think that they will be heard because of their many words. Do not be like them. Your Father knows what you need before you ask him. (Mt. 6:6–8)

In 1975, Fr. William Menninger also revived the practice of centering prayer, which has been described as "A method of refining intuitive faculties so that one can enter more easily into contemplative prayer."[8] It involves the repetition of the Jesus Prayer or sacred word(s), which facilitate inner silence. Like hesychastic prayer, we do not need to be a monk, hermit, or ascetic to practice centering prayer. All we need to do is detach interiorly from our words, thoughts, senses, and emotions, put our intellect and imagination aside for a time, come away from the world, and then be still and truly listen for the voice of God speaking in silence in our hearts. The similarities between centering prayer and Hesychastic prayer are striking, particularly with both having such a strong emphasis on entering into interior silence and experiencing the presence of God there. What was old is new once again.[9]

Furthermore, a "moment of silence" has been routinely practiced in many cultures as a moment of remembrance at occasional solemn events or even sometimes at joyous celebrations as we bring to mind God's presence among both the living and the deceased. This silence in that now moment is not seen as a vacuum, but as a sign of our quiet hope and our deepest desire for healing that will still any fears or anxious concerns. Historically, it has been understood by those gathered that silence will be the best form of suitable prayer for that occasion and that there can be no words at that time to express that which can only be interiorly heartfelt by those gathered. These moments of silence which recognize and acknowledge God's presence place a strong emphasis on interior stillness to bring oneself into the presence of God who is everywhere. Everywhere, of course, includes within our own self interiorly in the tranquil presence of the Holy Spirit who is our source of illumination.

In much the same way, centering prayer begins with the quieting down of our entire being holistically, so that we can open our hearts to enter into a period of interior silent prayer. We still our bodies, as well as the rational thoughts, feelings, or images that can flow from our minds. It is sacred space where we prepare our open heart to listen to the Lord who speaks in silence both within and without. Our role is to not so much have a conversation with God as to allow ourselves to develop a sense of intimate listening as we allow the Lord to control this time and what might occur during this time of interior prayer. It will move us beyond conversation to intimate communion with God. What will occur will not be an exchange of words as much as an exchange of hearts; Jesus' Sacred Heart will be in communion with our heart at the center of our being. Fr. Jean C. J. D' Elbee describes this in his widely known book *I Believe in Love*, which is based on the teachings of St. Therese of Lisieux, as "love for love" or what he calls "The Sublime Exchange," i.e., "My sins on Him, His blood on me."[10]

We are often used to conversation, much activity, and measurable productivity in our daily lives. That is how we usually spend our time. This will not be *our* time; this will be God's time. We turn our will over to God and any ideas about who we are and simply rest in the assurance that the Lord is everywhere, including at our center. He will show us that he is more interested in who we are becoming than who we are as we bring ourselves to him. We should not be so concerned with what happens during this "God time." The grace of God and the action of the Holy Spirit will accomplish all that God wills and wishes to accomplish. As was mentioned, it is helpful to have a sacred word(s) that we repeat more unconsciously than consciously to bring us to that interior sacred space. Most often, this sacred word can be a name for God (Abba, Jesus, Yahweh) or a characteristic of God (Holy Mystery, Merciful God, Holy Silence, Loving Father). Also, in a similar fashion to the hesychasts, some centering prayer devotees also recommend the repetition of the Jesus Prayer: "Lord Jesus have mercy on me, a sinner."[11]

We then allow these words to gently dismiss any thoughts, memories, anxieties, or fears. However, it is not enough to observe exterior silence; we must also strive for interior silence, that is, the quieting of the interior senses. This includes bad memories or imaginations, sensitive feelings, projected thoughts, bouts of depression and recollections of past hurts, useless worries about an uncertain future, or any other distractions, fears, or anxieties that we might encounter as we center ourselves and seek to enter that silent sacred space.

In this centering there will be a release of inner unconscious energy even though we will not be aware or conscious of this happening. Love of God, like all love we experience, has more to do with the choices of our hearts than it does with our consciousness. In the human person, love has primacy to any knowledge. The ultimate goal of centering prayer is loving intimacy, realized presence, and divine union with God at the center of our being. Psalm 46:10 tells us: "Be still and know that I am God."

When we meet God there at our center, our inner and outer worlds become united as deep calls to deep. This can be further envisioned as a transition from conversation with God to spiritual union with God in the Holy Spirit. Some mystical theologians have also called this form of prayer, "The Prayer of Quiet,"[12] as the soul experiences a profound sense of simple interior peace and rest in God's presence.

Centering familiarizes us with God's language which, as we have said, is silence. Advocates say it does not replace other prayer but encourages a deeper intimacy with God. Also, advocates of centering prayer say it helps them be more present and open to God, as it has been said: "Yesterday is history, tomorrow is mystery, today is a gift from God and that is why they call it the present."[13]

To keep it simple, we could say that there are four basic rules for anyone to enter into centering prayer:

1. Simply show up daily to spend time with God.
2. Let go and let God. This is God's time.
3. Forget your mind or any thoughts for a while and try to open your heart-center to God's presence.
4. Listen for what the Lord might be saying to you in silence at your center.

We will sometimes find that "simple" doesn't necessarily mean "easy." We should also realize that at our center, we will never become God. We only have been given the grace to become one with God as we move from conversation to mystical communion. Although we certainly can be interwoven with God at our center, in the fabric of our lives, God will always be "other" and remain transcendent.

Regarding the practice of centering prayer itself, one of its adherents, Fr. Basil Pennington of Spencer Abbey in Spencer, Massachusetts, outlines his four steps as follows:

1. Sit comfortably with your eyes closed, relax, and quiet yourself. Bring your love and faith to God.
2. Choose a sacred word that best supports your sincere intention to be in the Lord's presence and open to His divine action within you or keep repeating the "Jesus Prayer."
3. Let that word of prayer be gently present as the symbol of your sincere intention to be in the Lord's presence and open to His divine action within you. This prayer word is different than a mantra. It should only be used to lead us into the silence of the presence of God. The prayer word(s) becomes an intricate part of our very breathing which occurs mostly without our being conscious of it.
4. Whenever we become aware of anything (thoughts, feelings, perceptions, images, associations, etc.), simply return to your sacred word(s), your anchor.[14]

Fr. Thomas Keating, also of Spencer Abbey, another well-known and respected advocate of centering, adds this thought: "Centering prayer consists in letting go of every kind of thought during prayer, even the most devout thoughts." Centering is holistic. It involves our mental, spiritual, and physical self. It calms our emotions and slows our mind and our breathing to a point where we can "feel" a lot more going on inside us. It's like a state of "relaxed alertness."[15]

In the practice of centering, some people feel that it helps them to visualize a root system growing downwards from oneself. We visualize it growing down towards and into the earth further and further until it reaches way down into the earth below us, much like a "tree of life." It is from this centering in silence that any and all of our activity should begin and flow. If we practice this every day, we will essentially become what Ignatian spirituality refers to as "contemplatives in action."[16] We will no longer see silence as a void to be filled, but as an intricate part of our vital daily lifestyle.

Contemplation will allow us to renew our active lives (our work, our play, our study, and our relationships) so that all we do does not become unconscious action but rather gives glory to God. And the cycle will keep repeating itself each day. Our activity will regularly lead us into a time of silent prayer, and then we return to all activity with greater enthusiasm. Being a contemplative in action implies that our active life will feed off of our life of silent prayer and our prayer life will feed off of our active life. The cycle of contemplation and activity will never end for as long as we live.

NOTES

1. Rumi quotes, Good-Reads Quotes, https://www.goodreads.com/quotes/27617 -silence-is-the-language-of-god-all-else-is-poor.
2. F. Kaufman, ed., "Hesychasm," *New World Encyclopedia* (St. Paul, MN: Paragon House, 2009), https://www.newworldencyclopedia.org/entry/hesychasm.
3. St. John of the Cross, *The Dark Night of the Soul*, https://www.cccl.org/ccel/ john_cross/dark_night.toc.html.
4. "Jesus Prayer," Britannica (Chicago, IL: Encyclopedia Britannica, 2017), https: //www.britannica.com/topic/Jesus-prayer.
5. John Paul II, The Jesus Prayer, Pope John Paul II and the East Pope John Paul II. From *Eastern Theology Has Enriched the Whole Church* (Vatican City: L'Osservatore Romano, 1996). English translation, Rumkatkilise.org. Archived from the original on April 12, 2016, https://www.ewtn.com/catholicism/library/eastern-theology-has -enriched-the-whole-church-8802.
6. "Contemplative Prayer/Centering Prayer," Thomas Merton, Basil Pennington, Thomas Merton Society, http://www.thomasmertonsociety.org/Studia2/Pennington .pdf.
7. Thomas Merton, *Seven Storey Mountain, Contemplative Prayer* (New York: Harvest Books Division, Harcourt, 1948).
8. Fr. William Menninger, *The History of Centering Prayer* (West Milford, NJ" Contemplative Outreach Society, 1975), https://www.contemplativeoutreach.org/ history-of-centering-prayer/.
9. Thomas Keating, *Open Mind Open Heart* (London: Continuum, 1994), Section 34, Invitation #1.

10. Fr. Jean C. J. D'Elbee, *I Believe in Love* (Manchester, NH: Sophia Institute Press, 1974).

11. Ibid, Ch. 10, f. 3.

12. A. Devine, *Prayer of Quiet: In the Catholic Encyclopedia* (New York: Robert Appleton Company, 1911), New Advent Catholic Encyclopedia, http://www.newadvent.org/cathen/12608b.htm.

13. Attribution Alice Morse Earl et al., https://www.goodreads.com/quotes/search?q=Yesterday+is+history.+Tomorrow+is+a+mystery.+and+Today+is+a+gift.

14. Fr. Basil Pennington, *Centering Prayer, Renewing an Ancient Christian Prayer Form* (Garden City, NY: Image Books, Doubleday & Co, 1980).

15. Fr. Thomas Keating, *Open Mind, Open Heart* (Amity, NY: Amity House, 1986), p. 97.

16. St. Ignatius, *Introduction to Ignatian Spirituality*, "Contemplatives in Action" (Chicago: Loyola Press), https://www.loyolapress.com/catholic-resources/ignatian-spirituality/introduction-to-ignatian-spirituality/what-am-i-here-for-being-contemplatives-in-action/.

Chapter 11

Noise

We need to find God, and he cannot be found in noise and restlessness. God is the friend of silence. See how nature—trees, flowers, grass—grows in silence; see the stars, the moon, and the sun, how they move in silence. . . . We need silence to be able to touch souls.[1]—Mother Teresa

Noise is unwanted sound which may be considered unpleasant, distracting, or disruptive to hearing. Certain contributors to the overall noise problem are booming population growth, urban sprawl, inadequate noise regulations, technology, factory and industrial growth, and busier roads, airports, and highways. All the technology we've created, such as automobiles, cell phones, machines, construction and landscape equipment, aircraft, electronic devices, etc. now see to it that our world is constantly filled with an increasing level of noise. Loud music and other unwanted background noise can affect not only our hearing but also our ability to perceive or listen. All noise pollution affects not only our hearing and can be a constant annoyance, but over time, higher levels of noise can ultimately impact our overall health in a negative way. Noise stimulates the release of stress hormones in the brain. Healthwise, increased exposure to noise may cause or increase the likelihood of hearing loss, high blood pressure, heart disease, psychological disorders, sleep disturbances or deprivation, changes in brain chemistry, and even contribute to decreased work or educational performance. Noise is the antithesis of silence.

Even though we are aware of the harmful effects of noise, to most of the world, silence is just the absence of noise. It can be more than just that as well as more than soundlessness or wordlessness. To the Christian believer as well as many other religious faith traditions, silence is going to the inner heart-center of ourselves to listen to and subsequently to contemplate what God may be saying inside us. This is often referred to as the core of our being. It is here that we go beyond any past or future moment in time to be fully in the presence of God who is eternal and transcendent. At this God-centered place, which is beyond time or space, we meet the Holy Mystery of God who speaks in the language of silence and thus becomes for those of us who pray: Holy Silence. For our part in this quietude, we never think, imagine, or speak. We only listen. As said previously, this is the Lord's time.

In a particular Scripture passage in three of the Gospels (Mk. 4:35–41; Lk. 8:22–25; Mt. 8:23–27), Jesus is sound asleep in a fishing boat on the stormy and windswept sea. The terrified disciples wake him up and he stills their fears and doubts by telling the wind to be still and the stormy sea to be quiet and calm. In the same way today, Jesus can block out the whistling winds of fear, hurt, and anxiety blowing inside us and the noisiness of turbulent and stormy doubts that continually question our faith walk. Only Jesus can silence these noisy disturbances within us that often throw our faith completely off course. Once they are subdued, we can then return to prayer and meditation once again in the quiet, calm, peace, and tranquility Jesus will restore to our heart-center.

Unlike noise, silence and meditation can improve our mental and spiritual well-being. A conscious choice to put away technological devices and walk away from the noise and into the silence is a good start. All of these disruptions are not from outside influences. Some noise we create in ourselves with the thoughts and images that are the products of our own minds. First, on a daily basis, psychologists have calculated that the average person thinks about 6,000 thoughts per day.[2] That is a huge amount of thinking and even possibly enough to set our hair on fire. We need to create some space between our number of thoughts and an increased time for silence. Our inner voice can also create a significant amount of a noise-like distractions. We are so used to talking to others and even talking to God rather than listening that it can be difficult for us to turn off that outer or inner voice of ours. Silence is not simply a void to be filled; it needs to become for us a spiritual discipline that leads us into seeking the still small voice of God in prayer.

Distractions, chaos, stress, fears, anxiety, and many false gods will often try to keep us from finding God in the center of our being. Some of these idols might not even be very loud, but deviously subtle and invasive. These would include desire for approval, habitual vices, an unforgiving spirit, addiction to work, greed for gain, need for power or control, simmering anger, past hurts, resentment or grudges, and other various "noisemakers." These can create a dictatorial din which can distract us from listening for the voice of God speaking to us in the language of silence. The passage about Elijah in 1 Kings 19:11–13 comes to mind here:

Then the Lord said: Go out and stand on the mountain before the Lord; the Lord will pass by. There was a strong and violent wind rending the mountains and crushing rocks before the Lord—but the Lord was not in the wind; after the wind, an earthquake—but the Lord was not in the earthquake, after the earthquake, fire—but the Lord was not in the fire, after the fire, a light silent sound. When he heard this, Elijah hid his face in his cloak and went and stood at the entrance of the cave. (1 Kgs. 19:11–13)

Although various powerful, loud, and demonstrative phenomena such as strong wind, earthquakes, and fire can accompany the divine presence; they do not constitute the divine presence itself unlike the silent sound which is an unfathomable Holy Mystery containing the still small voice of God.

It is interesting, indeed, that as I begin to write this paragraph, a motorcycle seemingly without any muffler is revving up at a stop sign outside my window, and the noise is deafening to say the least, even with the window tightly closed. The noise and relentless chaos of our everyday life in this world can scar our souls, weigh down our spirits, and is a favored tool of the forces of evil to drown out the calming and tranquil voice of God. Sometimes, we even welcome this distraction to hide from the thoughts and feelings that cause us intense hurt or painful anxiety. Seeking silence is often one of the most basic tools at our disposal to subdue the noise occurring both inside and outside of ourselves. It provides a pathway for us to cut through the chaos and come face-to-face with our own negativity or the soul-stains of sinful issues. Only then can we enable ourselves to meet God in sacred space at our heart-center, to hear his voice speaking in silence, and then find our way to necessary purity, healing, and growth in the Holy Spirit.

In the C. S. Lewis classic novel *The Screwtape Letters*, the lead demon is a character called "Screwtape." He reveals to the reader one of the more interesting plans of the devil. To separate us from finding God at our center, one of the primary weapons the devil will choose to distract us is just simply "noise." Lewis even refers to the devil's kingdom as "The Kingdom of Noise." Satan, that wily coyote, knows that if we are distracted by noise that we will be unable to hear the voice of God in silence. Here is a glimpse into the devil's devious plan in the book as Screwtape's nephew, Wormwood, a less experienced junior tempter is told:

Music and silence—how I detest them both! How thankful we should be that ever since our Father entered Hell—though longer ago than humans, reckoning in light years, could express—no square inch of infernal space and no moment of infernal time has been surrendered to either of those abominable forces, but all has been occupied by Noise—Noise, the grand dynamism, the audible expression of all that is exultant, ruthless, and virile—noise which alone defends us from silly qualms, despairing scruples, and impossible desires. We will make the whole universe a noise in the end! We have already made great strides in this direction as regards the Earth. The melodies and silences of heaven will be shouted down in the end![3]

"A universe of noise" is an interesting demonic concept, particularly in light of the fact that the last chapter of this book, chapter 16, is titled "Silence of the Universe." Ironic, don't you think? In the United States today, adults now spend half a day each day on average interacting with media of all types.[4] Social media is actually a subtle form of the noise that exists in our world. It is a means of running away from our own reflective thoughts and tranquil prayer time. Fleeing from silence and the quiet stillness of active contemplation and meditation can even be considered symptomatic of a desire to flee from God. So, it may be time to turn off the television and satellite radio, mute the cell phone, stop the incessant texting, toss the tweets, close the computer, and ignore the internet. We should even tell ourselves that it is okay for us not to look at our email for a while. Besides, God is found only in the peaceful and still silence of "knee mail." Silence activates multiple parts of the brain and our central nervous system. It gives us time to turn down the inner noise created not only from outside of ourselves, but more often inside of ourselves. It can help us to increase awareness of what matters most. It cultivates recognition and appreciation of the present moment in time. A Jesuit priest who is a friend once told me: "Be present where you are." I never forgot those wise words.

In addition to contributing to our spiritual growth, silence has many mental and physical benefits as well. When we're frazzled or stressed and our nervous system is on overload, we can use the quiet stillness of a prayerful moment to tap into different parts of our nervous system that can help shut down our bodies' mental and physical responses. We are a whole self in its totality and cannot separate our body, soul, and spirit. Because we cannot compartmentalize ourselves, our mental, physical, and spiritual selves are all interconnected and we are affected by noise as an entire being.

Finally, during our prayer time, due to the level of noise going on outside of our prayer room, we could simply choose to physically get up and move ourselves to another quieter location. However, self-inflicted noise or noise going on inside of us is a different story as we will take that noise with us wherever we go. If the Lord isn't supplying us with any promptings from the Holy Spirit intended for our own benefit or given to speak to another person, then we should pray that the Lord would remove any obstacles, anxieties, or distractions. For our part, we should examine our conscience daily in an attempt to understand where our inner noise might be coming from while we continue to consistently set aside time each day to seek his tranquil presence. At the same time, we should continue to pray for the Lord to give the grace to overcome any of our interior noise as we try to listen for his still small voice speaking in the silence of our hearts.

Earlier in this chapter we discussed how noise is the fiendish friend of the devil and his legions. As we move into the next chapter of this book, titled "The Messianic Secret," we will see how the Lord Jesus demands silence from any and all of the demonic forces he encounters and overcomes as he exorcizes them. These forces of evil recognized Jesus as the Son of God right from the beginning of his public ministry. Therefore, because they could identify him, he demands their silence as we are told:

> He cured many who were sick with various diseases, and he drove out many demons, not permitting them to speak because they knew him. (Mk. 1:32–34)

NOTES

1. Mother Teresa, *Everyday Power, Inspiring Quotes by Mother Teresa on Kindness, Love, and Charity*, Quote #43 (New York: Everyday Power, 2021), https://everydaypower.com/quotes-by-mother-teresa/.

2. Jason Murdoch, "Humans Have More Than 6,000 Thoughts Per Day, Psychologists Discover," *Newsweek*, July 15, 2020, https://www.newsweek.com/humans-6000-thoughts-every-day-1517963.

3. C. S. Lewis, *Letter XXII, The Screwtape Letters* (New York: Collier, 1982), pp. 102–103.

4. "Time Flies: U.S. Adults Now Spend Nearly Half a Day Interacting with Media," Neilson Insights, July 31, 2018, www.nielsen.com/us/en/insights/article/2018/time-flies-us-adults-now-spend-nearly-half-a-day-interacting-with-media/.

Chapter 12

The Messianic Secret

WHAT IS A SECRET?

A secret, according to the definition of the word, is "something that is meant to be kept in silence or to be kept unknown, unheard, or unseen by others." Furthermore, it is meant to be kept from being made public knowledge or to become spread among several persons. The "secret keeper" who is charged with maintaining his or her silence in the matter is called a "confidant" or "confidante" and because the secret is a matter of faith or trust between two or more persons, the secret has the element of being "confidential" from the Latin meaning "with faith or trust." Additionally, there is involved the element of "mystery" because the secret is not or is yet to be revealed and therefore silence, concealment, and hiddenness are facets of it which must be maintained as a form of privacy among the parties involved.[1]

THE MESSIANIC SECRET

In the Gospels, particularly Mark's Gospel which was considered the first one actually written (not Matthew as in the Canon), there exists something called "The Messianic Secret." It centers on Jesus not wanting anyone to know his real identity beforehand and asking others for their silence in the matter of his being the Messiah. We find this first occurring immediately as Mark's Gospel opens in chapter one with Jesus demanding silence from the demons who knew Jesus was the Son of God:

> When it was evening, after sunset, they brought to him all who were ill or possessed by demons. The whole town was gathered at the door. He cured many

who were sick with various diseases, and he drove out many demons, not permitting them to speak because they knew him. (Mk. 1:32–34)

So, first the demons are exorcised, but they are told to remain silent and not to identify Jesus as the long-awaited Messiah and Son of God. Then as we drop down to verses 40–45 in chapter one, Jesus will cleanse a leper, but then warn him sternly not to reveal His identity and to keep it a secret:

A leper came to him [and kneeling down] begged him and said, "If you wish, you can make me clean." Moved with pity, he stretched out his hand, touched him, and said to him, "I do will it. Be made clean." The leprosy left him immediately, and he was made clean. Then, warning him sternly, he dismissed him at once. Then he said to him, "See that you tell no one anything, but go, show yourself to the priest and offer for your cleansing what Moses prescribed; that will be proof for them." The man went away and began to publicize the whole matter. He spread the report abroad so that it was impossible for Jesus to enter a town openly. He remained outside in deserted places, and people kept coming to him from everywhere. (Mk 1: 40–45)

So, what does the leper do after he was healed by Jesus? He immediately goes and tells *everybody*, proving that some people cannot remain silent in certain matters and just find it impossible to keep a secret a secret.

In Mark, chapter three, we find more demons recognizing Jesus as the Son of God and as they are exorcised, he sternly warns these unclean spirits to remain silent as well and not to reveal what was supposed to be kept secret for the time being. The demons were among the first to know Jesus' identity as the Messiah and he warns them sternly to keep this to themselves and not to make this known: "And whenever unclean spirits saw him, they would fall down before him and shout, 'You are the Son of God.' He warned them repeatedly not to make him known" (Mk. 3:11–12).

In Mark, chapter five, Jesus will warn the observing crowd in a likewise manner:

He took the child by the hand and said to her, "Talitha Koum," which means, "Little girl, I say to you, arise!" The girl, a child of twelve, arose immediately and walked around. [At that] they were utterly astounded. He gave strict orders that no one should know this and said that she should be given something to eat. (Mk. 5:41–43)

A little later in Mark, chapter seven, there is a similar occurrence where there is the healing of a deaf man and Jesus will warn the crowd similarly not to reveal His identity:

And people brought to him a deaf man who had a speech impediment and begged him to lay his hand on him. He took him off by himself away from the crowd. He put his finger into the man's ears and spitting, touched his tongue; then he looked up to heaven and groaned, and said to him, "Ephatha!" (that is, "Be opened!"). And [immediately] the man's ears were opened, his speech impediment was removed, and he spoke plainly. He ordered them not to tell anyone. But the more he ordered them not to, the more they proclaimed it. (Mk. 7:32–36)

Wow, what a well-kept secret, huh? And now the cat is going to really come out of the proverbial bag as Peter recognizes Jesus as the Messiah. This is the center point of Mark's Gospel. It is the high point and really considered as the climax. Storytellers and narrators refer to this high point by the French word, *denouement* which means: "The final part of a story, play, or narrative in which the strands of the plot are drawn together and matters which were heretofore kept silent, hidden, or unrevealed are then explained or resolved."[2] Everything from here on out after the climactic highpoint will race downhill toward the conclusion of the story. But as is the case with most story endings after the climax occurs, there will be a final twist or a final turnabout in the action before we get to the end of the story.

First, Jesus will warn Peter and the other disciples. He will ask them for their silence in the matter and for them not to tell anyone as he had previously warned others. This will occur in Mark, chapter eight. He will then warn them even more concerning keeping his Messianic role a secret after the transfiguration. This occurs as they come down from the mountain talking about Jesus soon to be rising from the dead in Mark, chapter nine. Here is the sequence that follows:

Now Jesus and his disciples set out for the villages of Caesarea Philippi.

Along the way he asked his disciples, "Who do people say that I am?" They said in reply, "John the Baptist, others Elijah, still others one of the prophets." And he asked them, "But who do you say that I am?" Peter said to him in reply, "You are the Messiah." Then he warned them not to tell anyone about him. (Mk. 8:27–30)

As they were coming down from the mountain, he charged them not to relate what they had seen to anyone, except when the Son of Man had risen from the dead. So, they kept the matter to themselves, questioning what rising from the dead meant. (Mk. 9:9–10)

The Messianic Secret in Mark's Gospel revolves around Jesus asking others for their silence and not wanting his full identity being made known and revealed until after the passion of the cross, which is soon to come. Certainly, His identity should remain a secret until after the resurrection when He rises from the dead as this mysterious "Son of Man" figure.[3] At this time, it will surely be made known that he is both Messiah as well as Son of God. It will then be no secret at that time because only God can rise from the dead or be the prime mover in causing others to rise from the dead.

Peter was right in calling Jesus the Messiah, but he misunderstood what the implication of that title was going to be. That's the twist in this Gospel story. Peter didn't understand that Jesus would also be the suffering servant described in 700 BC by the prophet Isaiah and that the path of discipleship will mean taking up the cross of the Lord. So, Peter will attempt to dissuade Jesus from going to the cross because Peter understands the meaning of Messiah to be something very different. Peter expects the Messiah-King to be someone who will come in mighty and awesome power, like a triumphant conquering hero. How Jesus, who is the hero of this story, will come in glory as the Messiah does not fully meet Peter's expectations. Soon the Messianic Secret will not remain shrouded in silence any longer and will disclose a very different kind of hero. At this time, Jesus will admonish Peter: "Get thee behind me Satan" (Mk. 8:33).

In his Gospel, Mark will depict Jesus as the anointed one, the Christ-Messiah, as well as the Son of Man. It is only after the resurrection that Jesus will be fully revealed as the Son of God. And this Messianic Secret is all wrapped up in the silence of the mystery with Jesus proclaiming that: "The Kingdom of God is in your midst." This in many ways will be a part of this well-kept secret; a secret which particularly concerned Jesus' identity. This is the Messianic Secret in the Gospel of Mark and that is why Jesus kept asking and demanding silence from the demons, the crowds, the lepers, and the disciples. It was Peter who first recognized Jesus as Israel's long-awaited Messiah. He was surely right; however, the Messiah would be someone very different from the Messiah that Peter and the nation of Israel had been expecting. In addition to being Messiah, Jesus would embody the suffering servant which was prophesied to come by Isaiah 700 years earlier. What follows are the words prophesied in the Old Testament Book of Isaiah long before Jesus was born:

> He bore the punishment that makes us whole, by his wounds we were healed. We had all gone astray like sheep, all following our own way; but the LORD laid upon him the guilt of us all. Though harshly treated, he submitted and did not open his mouth; Like a lamb led to slaughter or a sheep silent before shearers, he did not open his mouth. Seized and condemned, he was taken away. Who would have thought any more of his destiny? For he was cut off from the land of the living, struck for the sins of his people. He was given a grave among the wicked, a burial place with evildoers, though he had done no wrong, nor was

deceit found in his mouth. But it was the LORD's will to crush him with pain. By making his life as a reparation offering, he shall see his offspring, shall lengthen his days, and the LORD's will shall be accomplished through him. (Is. 53:4–10)

This appears to be the chief reason Jesus was asking for, and in some instances, demanding silence concerning his being the Messiah. It had to remain a Messianic Secret until the world could be shown God's revelation of just who the Messiah would be as Jesus, the hero, embodied this word. The final piece of the mystery, hidden in silence for so long, would be "revealed" (literally, lifting the veil) soon after the resurrection. The disciples of Jesus and the world would then come to realize that Jesus came not only to preach about the Kingdom of God, but that Jesus *was* and *is* the Kingdom of God. The Kingdom of God *was* and *is* in Jesus; therefore, he could say as recorded in Mark's Gospel: "The Kingdom of God *is* in your midst" (Mk. 1:15).

And finally, because of Jesus' real presence in the Eucharist and the Holy Spirit sent by Jesus being alive in us as believers in the church today, the Kingdom of God *is* still in our midst.[4] The difference is that now our silence is no longer required and we can go and tell everybody. The secret is out!

NOTES

1. "Secret," Merriam Webster, https://www.merriam-webster.com/dictionary/secret.

2. "Denouement," Ibid, Ch. 10, f. 3, https://www.britannica.com/art/denouement.

3. Michael Hickey, "Son of Man," *Themes from the Gospel of John* (Lanham, MD: Hamilton Books, 2021), pp. 157–160.

4. "The Real Presence of Jesus Christ in the Sacrament of the Eucharist: Basic Questions and Answers," United States Conference of Catholic Bishops, https://www.usccb.org/resources/The%20Real%20Presence%20of%20Jesus%20Christ%20in%20the%20Sacrament%20of%20the%20Eucharist.pdf.

Chapter 13

The Third Person

We believe in the Holy Spirit, the Lord, the giver of life.—"Nicene Creed"[1]

In faith, we believe in the Holy Trinity, three persons in one God: Father, Son, and Holy Spirit.[2] This is an Absolute Mystery in the true sense of the word shrouded in silence, which can only be envisioned by proposing figures of speech and analogies such as similes or metaphors. The Trinity cannot be fully comprehended theologically or understood completely through the use of reason or logic alone. It is not a puzzle, riddle, or enigma to be solved or an obscure or ambiguous question because these can be solved ultimately by reason and logic. The Trinity is Absolute Mystery and Absolute Truth in the sense that even though it is revealed to us, we cannot fully grasp it through the use of our finite minds. What we do understand about the Trinity appears out there on the horizon, but as soon as we move closer to the horizon, another horizon opens up for us. Mystery is the ground of reality, so beyond the revelation of the Trinity is the much greater unrevealed mystery where God only speaks to us in silence.

In the Trinity, there is One God in three persons, however, even the terms "Father" and "Son" can be seen as more "personal." Part of our difficulty in fully recognizing the Holy Spirit as a person is compounded by the many symbols in the Bible for the third person of the Trinity: i.e., water, anointing oil, fire, wind, breath, cloud, the seal, the dove, and the Paraclete. Apart from these ancient biblical models and to symbolize the Holy Spirit in more modern terms, Fr. John Unni, the Pastor of St Cecelia's Church in Boston, Massachusetts, among others, has likened the Holy Spirit to "Our Divine GPS."[3] Of course, these metaphorical terms all serve to reflect something about the identity of the Holy Spirit, but they do not specifically help us to see the Holy Spirit as a person, i.e., the third person of the Trinity.

The Father is the source of all things and first spoke through creation. The Father then spoke indirectly to Moses, revealing His name as *Yahweh*, "I Am

Who I Am."[4] He then spoke fully and directly through his only Son who was born in the fullness of time. The Son, Jesus Christ, born of the Holy Spirit and Mary, the virgin Mother of God, first spoke through his birth, followed by his signs and wonders. Then like a silent lamb led to slaughter, He primarily and ultimately spoke through his dying on the cross and rising. The Father then sent the Holy Spirit who came into the world from the Father and through the Son. The Gospels tell us that Jesus was "conceived by the Holy Spirit and born of the Virgin Mary" (Mt. 1:18–23; Lk. 1:30–35; *Apostles' Creed*).[5] Furthermore, "The Holy Spirit descended on Jesus like a dove during his baptism" (Jn. 1:32; Lk. 3:22). In his Farewell Discourse after the Last Supper, Jesus promised to "send the Holy Spirit" to his disciples after his departure (Jn. 17:1–26). The Holy Spirit was to be "another Paraclete" as Jesus was the first Paraclete.

We now live in the age of the Holy Spirit who speaks primarily through the Christian church in the modern world. This church was born on Pentecost as Mary, the Mother of God, and the apostles were gathered together in the upper room where they all became filled with the outpouring of the Holy Spirit. Today all professed and baptized Christians as members of this church on earth have received some portion of the Holy Spirit. The Trinity is One God in three persons. That being the case, if we are in union with the Father, the Son, and the Holy Spirit at our time and place in the procession of history, then we are living "in the Spirit." The church, as a Sacrament of the Kingdom of God, is the deposit of the Holy Spirit, but the Holy Spirit has no "name" and is certainly the most mysterious member of the Godhead. Although the Holy Spirit has been called "advocate," "comforter," "consoler," "counselor," and "Paraclete," to name a few, none of these are personal "names" as we know them.[6] The Father has been called "Yahweh" and the Son has been called "Jesus," but the Bible never once gives a singular identifying name to the third person of the Trinity. Unlike Jesus, there is no evidence that the Holy Spirit has become any individual person with a human body or an identifying personal name. If the church is the deposit of the Holy Spirit consisting of many persons who are the people of God, then how are we to understand who is the Holy Spirit? Exactly who and what is the Holy Spirit still remains as one of the deepest mysteries of the Trinity. The mystery of the Holy Spirit remains shrouded and hidden in almost complete silence to this day.

In fact, the word "mystery" itself came into our language from the Greek *mysterion,* which meant "to shut or hide." It signifies something which is unknowable or valuable knowledge which is kept secret. It is rooted in the Greek word *mystos* which means "keeping silence" or "closed lips." All of these words appear several times in the Bible, as does another Greek word, *apocolypsis*, which means "revelation," or, more literally, "lifting the veil." The Gospel writers and the Apostle Paul would use these words often to apply to the divine plan of God or when speaking about Divine Revelation which had heretofore been kept secret, but now revealed through Jesus Christ and made public with the salvation of humankind as its object. The Holy Spirit, though intimately involved in the divine plan of God, still remains very much a mystery wrapped in silence and hidden "behind the veil" of the Divine Revelation of God.

If Jesus Christ is the Sacrament of God, the church is the Sacrament of the Kingdom of God, and every baptized Christian in the church has received some measure of the Holy Spirit, then unless any one person might receive the fullness of the Holy Spirit as Jesus had, the Holy Spirit cannot possibly be identified with any one individual person. The third person of the Trinity must remain as the Spirit of Jesus Christ sent from the Father through the Son, spread among all of us who are baptized into the church, which is the deposit of the Holy Spirit on earth until the end of time. The Holy Spirit now lives in all of us who are living a life in the spirit as God's presence among His people.

Although the Holy Spirit remains shrouded in mystery, we do know that a few people on earth have been close to the Holy Spirit. First, Mary, the Mother of God, gave birth through the Holy Spirit. Then John the Baptist recognized the descent of the Holy Spirit in the form of a dove upon Jesus and prophesied that Jesus would baptize with the Holy Spirit and fire. Jesus was filled with the Holy Spirit from birth and sent the Holy Spirit through his dying and rising. Mary and the chosen apostles were gathered in the upper room as the Holy Spirit descended upon the church. So, the more we know about any of their lives, the closer we will come to recognizing the personal presence of the Holy Spirit.

The Holy Spirit is the Spirit of Jesus Christ and is love incarnate. The true measure of any one individual having received the Holy Spirit still remains as the manifestation of "the fruit of the Spirit" in their life. We have been told in the Bible that

> The fruit of the Spirit is love, joy, peace, patience, kindness, generosity, faithfulness, gentleness, and self-control. (Gal. 5:22)

Recognizing this in the life of any individual is recognition of the Holy Spirit. The "fruit of the Spirit" is meant to imply a single fruit—the Greek term used in the Bible is singular and not the plural, i.e., "fruits." This is not a list of nine separate fruits but nine characteristics of the (single) fruit of the Spirit. It is love which begins and flows unconditionally and selflessly in Christ. Those who profess to know and walk with the Holy Spirit, the Spirit of Jesus Christ, must demonstrate this fruit to the world in quiet and self-sacrificing, but nonetheless, very concrete, ways. All fruit of the Holy Spirit begins and ends with love. The scriptures call this kind of love, *agape*.

As has been discussed previously, *agape* is God's love given to man as the grace and gift of the Father. It is mature, dynamic, Christian love activated by the Holy Spirit and rooted in the life, death, and resurrection of Jesus Christ. It is beyond lust, eroticism, self-fulfilling union, affection, friendship, or brotherly-sisterly love. *Agape* is humble and total dedication, self-sacrifice, and devotion to another unconditionally. There is no extent or limit to the personal cost. God is pure uncreated being, thus encompassing and including every individual created person, place, matter, power, and force, essentially all of creation. So, the more we see this love and its fruit in any one individual as a created being, the more the Holy Spirit is silently present in the power of love and the Holy Spirit becomes in fact, "personified" together with the other persons of the Trinity, the Father and the Son.

The Gospel of Jesus Christ offers us a paradox, in that we must choose to die to self for the Holy Spirit in us to grow and become more "personified." Others will see the presence of the Holy Spirit as we begin to bear more fruit. In particular, we will manifest God's love and demonstrate that love to others. Because "God is love" (1 Jn. 4), *agape* is God's essence, and the Lord wants us to come to know and experience his perfect nature. This is not something conceptual. We come to know and experience the "essential love" (that being such by its essence) of God through knowing the Holy Spirit who is the Spirit of Truth. The more we know the Holy Spirit, the more we will manifest the fruit of the Spirit (Gal. 5:22) and love others and love God who loved us first. In 1 John the scriptures tell us:

> We belong to God, and anyone who knows God listens to us, while anyone who does not belong to God refuses to hear us. This is how we know the Spirit of Truth and the spirit of deceit. Beloved, let us love one another, because love is of God; everyone who loves is begotten by God and knows God. Whoever is without love does not know God, for God is love. In this way the love of God was revealed to us: God sent his only Son into the world so that we might have life through him. In this is love: not that we have loved God, but that he loved us and sent his Son as expiation for our sins. Beloved, if God so loved us, we also must love one another. No one has ever seen God. Yet, if we love one another, God remains in us, and his love is brought to perfection in us. This is how we know that we remain in him and he in us, that he has given us of his Spirit. (1 Jn. 4:6–13)

Agape can also be called "Eucharistic love" because if we know the Holy Spirit at the heart of our being, we will know the Lord's real presence there, ready to speak to us in prayerful silence. When we know this kind of love, the Holy Spirit will also manifest the fruit of the Spirit (Gal. 5:22) in our lives, though the mystery will still remain veiled and not fully revealed to us in its totality.[7]

Finally, any mystery is a question and questions do not always give us immediate answers. Sometimes our questions will only lead us on to bigger questions. With some of life's bigger questions, in faith we can only take them to God in prayer. There we can ask: "Who is the Holy Spirit?" With this question we may find, as we are asking it of God who will speak to us in the silence of our hearts, simultaneously God might be asking a similar question of us: "Can you become this person?" Then in prayer, our conversation might become muted once again as we will probably have no more words and then seek only God's voice in prayer who will speak to us once again in the language of Holy Silence.

"My best daily prayer, apart from the Mass and breviary, continues to be simply, 'Come, Holy Spirit.'" (Fr. Theodore Hesburgh)

It is said of Fr. Hesburgh, the late president of Notre Dame University, that after saying the closing prayer "Come Holy Spirit" each and every morning, he would complete it by saying the words,

"Okay now, let's be on our way."[8]

NOTES

1. "Nicene Creed," United States Conference of Catholic Bishops, https://www.usccb.org/beliefs-and-teachings/what-we-believe.

2. "Mystery of the Most Holy Trinity," Ibid, Ch. 13, f. 1, https://bible.usccb.org/bible/readings/053021.cfm See also https://www.usccb.org/catechism/pt1sect2chpt1art1p2.

3. "Divine GPS," Rev. John Unni, Homily, St. Cecelia's Parish, Boston, Massachusetts, January 9, 2022.

4. "Yahweh," "I Am Who I Am," (Ex. 3: 14–15), Ibid, Ch. 1, f. 3.

5. Ibid, Ch. 1, f. 3; see also "Apostles Creed," United States Conference of Catholic Bishops, https://www.usccb.org/prayer-and-worship/prayers-and-devotions/prayers/basic-prayers.

6. Ibid, Ch. 1, f. 3 (Jn. Ch. 14–16); see also Michael Hickey, "Spirit, Paraclete, and Truth," *Themes from the Gospel of John* (Lanham MD: Hamilton Books, 2021), pp. 165–170.

7. "Agape," see Ch. 15; see also "Agape" in *Catholic Encyclopedia* (New York: Robert Appleton Company, 2022), https://www.newadvent.org/cathen/01200b.htm.

8. "Holy Spirit Prayer," Fr. Theodore Hesburgh, University of Notre Dame, https://hesburgh.nd.edu/fr-teds-life/an-extraordinary-life/in-his-own-words/hesburgh-quotes/.

Chapter 14

Death

The Lord will destroy the veil that veils all peoples. He will destroy death forever.—Is. 25:7–8

DEATH OF A LOVED ONE

Most of us would rather die a hundred deaths than to experience the death of someone we love deeply. A loved one's death is often a time of great personal pain for those left behind. That day frequently comes like an uninvited interloper, robbing us of the love and intimacy we shared with that person who cannot ever be replaced. After the many tears and grieving, it leaves a soul-searing silence unlike any other. The silence left by that person is all-encompassing and envelops us as their memories are all around us. In terms of an earthly relationship with the one we love, there is no more today or tomorrow, there is only yesterday. The residual vacuum is a testimony that something unsurpassable and totally radical has happened to the one we love and to us as well. Only the silence which remains can speak to the depths of our woundedness. All words become useless in our attempt to define, understand, or explain away the reality. Others can try to comfort us by assuring us that they are there for us at that time and we are not alone, but it is not enough. It is we who are left to listen as we are locked away within the confines of that fathomless abyss.

The closeness we had with that person who was alive and present in our lives leaves a tremendous void which can then only be filled by becoming closer to God. At that time in our life, God's presence can often become more necessary, intense, and immediate. The late Catholic theologian, Karl Rahner, writing on the *Theology of Death* in 1958, maintained that God's closeness to the whole of creation underlined his concept of death and dying. Rahner proposed that "Grace, as God's self-communication, presents death not as a punishment but as a two-sided opportunity: intensifying the relationship between the human person and God."[1] And as said so simply and succinctly in John's Gospel by the Apostle Peter: "Lord, to whom shall we go? You have the words of eternal life" (Jn. 6:68).

In many ways, earthly death separates us physically from those we love in this life. So, first of all, death can be some form of separation from one we loved and who loved us. If we believe in faith that all life is in God, and if we truly believe that our loved one has gone "home to God," then the only way at that time we can get any closer to those we loved who have died their earthly death is to get closer to God. Consequently, the only way we can get closer to God is to enter into the sacred silence where God is present. There in prayer, we find that both God and the person we loved in this life are both present to us and are alive for He has told us:

> That the dead will rise even Moses made known in the passage about the bush, when he called "The Lord" the God of Abraham, the God of Isaac, and the God of Jacob; He is not God of the dead, but of the living, for to him all are alive. (Lk. 20:37–38)

Are these just words for us or do we believe Jesus, who said them?

DEATH, LIFE, AND SILENCE

> Silence before being born, silence after death: life is nothing but noise between two unfathomable silences.—Isabel Allende[2]

Hopefully, most of us would not adopt as our own the completely fatalistic viewpoint which seems to be inherent in the above quotation on death, life, and silence. But all human possibility and potential must be viewed in the context of death as an earthly finality and an eventual "deadline" which we all must meet. Death is for all of us a limiting horizon and a natural and eventual end to the life we previously had on this earth since our own human birth. Even though we acknowledge that everyone must die, we put off our own personal death out into some indefinite future. But the death of others forces us to confront our own earthly finality. It also forces us to see beyond any horizon of a meaningless, futile, and future existence of a lifeless everlasting silence.

On the one hand, we cannot deny that our time on this planet will reach its culmination in our own earthly death. We are and will be "dust" as the Scripture tells us (Gen. 3:19), but on the other hand, we are called to believe in faith that we will eventually be "beloved dust." In many ways defining "death" might be as difficult as defining "life" (at least in terms of reaching a consensus or a unifying definition of terms). As related to human death, we might say that in terms of stating a common dictionary definition, "death" could be defined by many as "the permanent and irreversible cessation of any individual's biological functions."[3] Even simply stating that, however, would leave it subject to various and qualifying religious, legal, medical, and scientific opinions.

In the Old Testament of the Bible, the death of any person had to do with the departure of what was considered to be their "vital force" (1 Kgs. 17:21). With the ensuing writings of Plato, Aristotle, and other philosophers who followed prior to the birth of Christ, the concept of body and soul became more evident.[4] By the time of the writings of the New Testament Gospels, the idea began to be established that the principle of life is the spirit and soul. Death became thought of as "giving up the spirit." We find in the description of Jesus' death on the cross: "Jesus cried out in a loud voice and then gave up his spirit" (Mt. 27:50). In many of the Apostle Paul's letters, death might also be seen as being more than a physical bodily death or the separation of body and soul. It would be primarily a spiritual separation from God, the source of all life (Rom. 5:14–21, 6:21–23, 8:2–6).

In defining "death," the crux of the problem initially arises with how each of us might define "life," what life is, when life begins, and when life ends—or even if it ever ends. On the other hand, I think we might find some agreement in saying that our human death does bring about a personal earthly silence for each person who passes through its earthly gate. Of course, even this would not include the silence of other persons or things related to the memory of that particular person, and only the earthly silence of that individual person. Therefore, even that statement could in some ways be problematic. Perhaps the best thing we could safely say in seeking agreement and consensus is that in many ways "death," "life," and "silence" are merely words. These words stand on the cusp between the seen and unseen. Therefore, their meaning as a reality can only be grounded in mystery which is the ground of all reality. Nothing can be fully confirmed or defined as regards their full meaning without the questioner as a person having actually died and had an experience of their own individual and extremely personal earthly death.

Furthermore, we as Christians believe that our own death will bring not so much a finality or a silence to our life as much as a necessary and transformative change. We would also say that our evolving relationship to our own true self, to others, to the universe, and to God, is essentially tied to the life, death, and resurrection of Jesus Christ. Death, we are told, is the consequence of sin (Gen. 2–3), and it is sin which led to death. But Jesus has conquered sin and thus deprived death of its power in and through his dying and rising from death. The scriptures tell us: "The last enemy to be destroyed is death" (1 Cor. 15:26) and "To die with Christ is to live with Christ" (Rom. 6:8). Only through his death would Jesus be able to send the Holy Spirit who is the new presence of Christ in the world and is alive in us as a community of believers.

The last book of the Bible, the Book of Revelation, tells us that prior to our death, the manner in which we have lived out our earthly existence will accompany us through our own earthly death. If we die in the Lord, the way we have lived our life on this earth will speak for us out of the silence in ways that no words could ever speak on our behalf. Here we are told by a voice from heaven:

> I heard a voice from heaven say, "Write this: Blessed are the dead who die in the Lord from now on." "Yes," said the Spirit, "let them find rest from their labors, for their works accompany them." (Rev. 14:13)

Finally, one of my favorite poems as regards the subject of death and dying has always been *Gone from My Sight*, written by American poet Henry Van Dyke in the mid-1800s.[5]

GONE FROM MY SIGHT

> I am standing upon the seashore. A ship, at my side,
> spreads her white sails to the moving breeze and starts
> for the blue ocean. She is an object of beauty and strength.
> I stand and watch her until, at length, she hangs like a speck
> of white cloud just where the sea and sky come to mingle with each
> other.
>
> Then, someone at my side says, "There, she is gone."
>
> Gone where?
>
> Gone from my sight. That is all. She is just as large in mast,
> hull and spar as she was when she left my side.
> And, she is just as able to bear her load of living freight to her des-
> tined port.
> Her diminished size is in me—not in her.
>
> And, just at the moment when someone says, "There, she is gone,"
> there are other eyes watching her coming, and other voices
> ready to take up the glad shout, "Here she comes!"
>
> And that is dying . . .

One day all whom we love, as well as our own selves, will be transferred from the silence of death into the love, peace, and serenity of eternity. We will then die only to death and live in love eternally. For each of us, the pathway from death to life will be as unfamiliar, narrow, dark, and silent as the uterine birth canal of our mother who first brought us to birth and gave us life. So, may the words of Isaiah's Old Testament prophecy, which were quoted at the beginning of this discussion on the silence of death, find their eventual fulfillment in our own personal experience of sharing in Christ's resurrection from the dead. This victory of the love of Christ over death has been promised us in the words of Paul from the New Testament book of First Corinthians:

> When the perishable has been clothed with the imperishable, and the mortal with immortality, then the saying that is written will come true: "Death has been swallowed up in victory." (1 Cor. 15:54; Is. 25:8)

NOTES

1. Karl Rahner and C. H. Henkey, trans., *The Theology of Death* (Freiburg: Crossroads Publishing, Herder and Herder, 1972), pp. 1–127.

2. Isabel Allende, "Death, Life, and Silence" Inspiring Quotes, https://www .inspiringquotes.us/quotes/sXWw doHwcY1F.

3. Ibid, Ch. 10, f. 3, "Death," *Encyclopedia Britannica*, https://www.britannica .com/science/death.

4. Plato et al., "Philosophy of Death," E. Zalta, ed., *Stanford Encyclopedia of Philosophy* (Stanford, CA: Stanford University Press, 2018), https://plato.stanford.edu/.

5. Henry Van Dyke, "Gone from my Sight," All Poetry, https://allpoetry.com/Gone -From-My-Sight.

Chapter 15

Love

The perfection of the Christian life consists in love. First and foremost, in the love of God, then in the love of neighbor. The love that God has for us infuses and creates the goodness which is present in all things.— Thomas Aquinas[1]

THE LOVE OF GOD IS UNIVERSAL AND PERSONAL

God's universal love is boundless and limitless. It is love intended to be seen in everything around us and experienced personally by everyone, although some feel they are beyond God's loving reach. Its direct effect is for us to feel lovingly held, as if we were being infinitely caressed by the loving arms of the universe. Universal love tends toward universal consciousness and self-consciousness whose center is Christ consciousness.

It was the spiritual writer and theologian Fr. Henri Nouwen, in borrowing from the modern theologies of Jesuits Teilhard de Chardin and Karl Rahner, who is quoted as saying: "What is most personal is most universal and what is most universal is most personal."[2] This can be seen as a theological basis for the Universal Christ being first personified in Jesus of Nazareth. Christ is God's complete offer of self-communication which has both personal and universal implications in that it is salvific for the whole of reality and all humankind as the universe evolves and is drawn toward divine love. Sadly, this universal grace and the gift of divine love can freely be refused by those who personally choose to do so.

At the heart of the universality of Christ is the unconditional self-sacrificing love of God for each and every human person. This makes the universal personal. This love was made real and manifest in the life, death, resurrection, and ascension of Jesus Christ who died and rose not just for everyone, but for you and me personally.

The Scriptures tell us: "God is love" (1 Jn. 4:8, 16). The unification, harmony, order, and love by which the universe was created has been centered in Christ. His presence in the universe gives all of reality its Christic dimension. The silence of the universe has been filled with the Logos (The Word of God), spoken into the universe by God the Father. In the Incarnation, through his crucifixion and resurrection, the person Jesus of Nazareth would become the Universal Christ. This Christ event filled the universe with the love of God in the Holy Spirit sent by the Father, through the Son, and is now alive in each one of us who is a member of the Body of Christ.

Furthermore, because the Holy Spirit is in us, when we act in love personally, whether it be in big ways or small, it has universal implications because we touch the lives of others with God's Spirit. God's essence is universal love, and we only have to personally cooperate with the grace which is offered and die to self. The Holy Spirit will then take possession of our spirit and draw us personally and silently into the mystery of universal love.

The Greek word, *mysterion* (mystery), means "to shut or hide." It is rooted in the Greek words *mystos* which means "keeping silence" and *myein* which means "closed lips."[3] The mystery of the Universal Christ continues to be revealed as the universe evolves. Love is the strongest power in the universe; it is expansive and eternal, and love is all there is in the end (1 Cor. 13:13). The end will only occur after all humanity is reconciled to God in Christ and God becomes all in all.

As is discussed in chapter 13 on the Holy Spirit, the early Christian writers and theologians called this type of love *agape* (Gk.) to distinguish it from other types of love such as *eros* (Gk., eroticism) or *philia* (Gk., affection), which were considered lower forms. *Agape* is the highest form of love which originated in God's covenantal love for humankind and extended to human persons. Its origin is divine, and it is an unconditional and self-sacrificing type of love. It passionately seeks the good of the other and includes, but transcends, all desires, feelings, and emotions.

Without the grace and gift of God's love for human persons, love would be reduced to a mixture of mere sentimentality, pleasures, jealousy, and competition. It would ultimately seek sexual domination and exploitation and its essence would be tarnished by our self-seeking pride. It would be virtue-less, filled with self-centeredness and the desire to control, manipulate, and possess the other. Left to its own devices, humanity would create a love devoid of beauty, goodness, passion, perfect essence, and self-sacrificing presence— all of which have their source and end in God. This eternal and unconditional love was given to us as the grace and gift of a loving God in the incarnation of Jesus Christ. God's love seeks union and thus creates a Christocentric universe which had its beginning and, ultimately, will find its end in love. Like the poet Dante, Jesuit Theologian Teilhard de Chardin believed that "It is love which moves the sun and all the other stars."[4] Teilhard described love in the following words: "Love is the most universal and mysterious of cosmic energies. . . . It is primitive and universal psychic energy—the very blood of spiritual evolution."[5] We, like the dynamic and evolving universe that we are a part of, are not just human beings but a dynamic human becoming. Because God is an uncreated being and the primordial storyteller, no other love story or storyteller could ever tell us who we are or who we are becoming in Christ. Let us never forget God's gift and attempt to remake ourselves in the image of any other lover than our "Eucharistic lover."

In Greek mythology, the story of King Midas found in Ovid's *Metamorphoses XI* comes to mind here.[6] Rather than accept the beauty, love, and goodness he found in the universe as it existed, this king loved gold so much that he wished that everything he touched would turn to gold. His heart's desire and what he thought he loved turned out to be a curse and not a blessing. He turned his roses into gold and found them lacking in their rich beauty, and they had lost their fragrance. His food and drink turned to gold when he touched them, and he nearly died of hunger and thirst. He even turned his daughter into gold when he touched her hand, and she became lifeless. Consequently, King Midas came to hate the plenteous gold he thought he loved and prayed to his god to remove the curse. This story from folklore is reminiscent of how unhappy we would be with anything less than the perfect love God has gifted us with and asked us to imitate. Our God is alive in the Holy Spirit and wishes to convey his perfect love in prayer at our heart-center. Perhaps a first step for us would be to listen to His loving words spoken in silence and to recognize that unlike what King Midas might have imagined, God's "silence is more than golden."[7]

The story of the universe is an old story with a very long history, but it is also a story within a much older story—that being the story of universal and personal love. This love originated and was sent from God the Father and became alive as the Holy Spirit of Jesus Christ who now lives in each of us personally as a member of the Body of Christ. Like the compass always pointing to the true north, the Holy Spirit alive in us will always point to the Head, the Universal Christ, who waits for us at our future conclusion of this universal yet very personal love story.[8]

THE SILENT MYSTERY OF LOVE

When two persons are in love, no words are necessary. They are content to simply gaze into each other's eyes or faces as a silent expression of their love. Even the words "gape" or "a-gape" in the English language, which were derived originally from the Greek word *agape,* have now come to mean "to look at someone or something with your mouth wide open in wordless awe or wonder."[9]

God lives as the mystery of love within persons and is a spiritual dynamism that draws us away from our own reality and into the silent mystery who is totally other and a transcendent reality. As was said earlier, God is love's source and end; it is God's essence and existence. God is totally other. Our love of God cannot be separated from the love of "an-other" person. Love loses its spiritual dynamism and energy if it tries to remain anonymous. We cannot really love without loving at least one other person. So, being "in love" as part of this silent mystery must be experienced. Therefore, loving has primacy to any knowing including knowledge of the love of God.

As "imperfect saints" our essence and existence is less than perfect love and the only way we can orient ourselves to God's perfect love is to become part of this silent mystery and love an-other or others. Although love is universal in that God is its source and end, when we love another, love becomes most personal. Love then assumes a face and a "person-ality." If we believe that love has its source and end in God, when we love another person, we move in the spirit of love which is oriented toward its spiritual union with the God of the universe.

The Holy Spirit alive in us always points to Christ and is the giver of life and true love. God looks at us from the perspective of eternal love. We experience God's enduring love for us at our heart-center where God's Sacred Heart can speak to our heart in God's language which is silence. The goal of our life should be to receive and give Holy Spirit love which can only come primarily through spending time with the Lord in prayerful silence. In the end, it will be this Holy Spirit love in us and others which will prove to be stronger than death.

One of the greatest epic poems ever written was *The Divine Comedy* by Dante,[10] which was briefly mentioned earlier. To Dante, love has to do with every movement in the universe—from small human choices to the cosmic movement of the stars and planets. All are motivated by love. And it is the love of God which gives the entire universe its proper order as everything moves according to God's will. In the poem, Dante continually moves back and forth in focusing on two kinds of love—human love and divine love. He sees human love as the love shared between human beings and divine love as being God's love. God appears to Dante as three equally large circles occupying the same space representing the Father, the Son, and the Holy Spirit, and divine love is seen by Dante as symbolized in Paradise by an enormous rose.

With Dante's enormous rose, the symbol of divine love in mind, let me say that one of my favorite contemporary songs has always been *The Rose,*[11] sung by Bette Midler, Amanda McBroom, and others. It puts to song the relationship between the seed of love and the flower of life found in the beauty of the rose. Before it can flower, the rose must begin from a tiny seed which contains in its memory bank all of what it will take to create the rose. But the seed must be sown in the ground and die first, otherwise it cannot flower. Jesus of Nazareth is the seed of God's love. On the cross of Christ that seed flowered into an enormous rose that filled the entire universe with divine love, as so aptly stated in the lyrics of *The Rose*:

> Love. It is a flower,
> And you its only seed.

The previous chapter, on death, concerned the earthly finality of death and the deafening silence it leaves for those of us left behind. Let me say, in conclusion, that our human death cannot be seen as the final ending of the love which is in us, of our being in love, or of our loving reality. We will continue to move with the Holy Spirit in the direction of love, which is in Christ in God, and is expansive and never ends (1 Cor. 13:13). Although death may be our final earthly reality, universal love will remain as the ultimate reality. Therefore, in the circle of love, our human death cannot lead to that which is un-love, un-being, or un-reality. The circle of love will ultimately lead us to, what Dante described as the three circles occupying the same space. The source and end of universal love is God—Father, Son, and Holy Spirit. The Trinity is now for us a Holy Mystery, whose presence can be experienced by us personally, as we love others here on earth. That love will continue to grow and flower as we enter prayerfully into the Holy Silence each day. There we can listen for God's voice speaking, and then empowering the Holy Spirit in us to give us the grace to show us the way to love more perfectly. For as the Apostle Paul tells us in 1 Corinthians 13:

> When the perfect comes, the partial will pass away. . . . There are in the end three things that will last, faith, hope, and love, and the greatest of these is love. (1 Cor. 13:10, 13)

NOTES

1. Thomas Aquinas, *Summa Theologica*, Q 184, A. 3, "On the State of Perfection," https://www.ccel.org/ccel/aquinas/summa.SS_Q184_A3.html.
2. Henri Nouwen, "What Is Most Personal Is Most Universal," Henri Nouwen Society, 2018, https://henrinouwen.org/meditations/what-is-most-personal-is-most-universal/.
3. "Mystery," Etymology Online, https://www.etymonline.com/word/mystery.

4. Dante Alighieri, *The Divine Comedy, Canto Paradiso 33* (New York: Columbia University Press, 2022), https://digitaldante.columbia.edu/dante/divine-comedy/paradiso/paradiso-33/.

5. Teilhard De Chardin, *The Spirit of the Earth* (San Francisco, CA: S.N. Pub., Internet Archive, 1936, VI, 32–34 E; 40–42).

6. Ovid, *Metamorphoses XI, 85–105*, King Midas and the Golden Touch, https://ovid.lib.virginia.edu/trans/Metamorph11.htm#485520963.

7. "Silence Is golden," Merriam-Webster, https://www.merriam-webster.com/dictionary/silence%20is%20golden.

8. Raymond E. Brown, Joseph A. Fitzmeyer, Roland E. Murphy, and Carlo Maria Cardinal Martini, ed., *The New Jerome Biblical Commentary* (Englewood Cliffs, NJ: Prentice-Hall, 1990), Sec. 79:22, 33, 40.

9. "Gape, Agape," Ibid, Ch. 15, f. 3, https://www.etymonline.com/word/gape#:~:text=gape%20(v.),the%20mouth%2C%22%20from%201530s.

10. Ibid, Ch. 15, f. 4.

11. Bette Midler, *The Rose*, Lyrics Online, https://www.lyrics.com/lyric/14448361/Bette+Midler/The+Rose.

Chapter 16

Silence of the Universe

Waves of thought arise from the ocean of wisdom; they assume the forms of sound and speech and then cast themselves back into the ocean.—Rumi[1]

REALITY AND MEANING

Reality is the quality or state of being real, genuine, and authentic. It has a basis in fact and truth. It includes everything that is, no matter whether observable or comprehensible, visible, or invisible. Reality is far more complex than what our immediate sense experience can tell us. The senses of seeing, hearing, tasting, touching, and smelling provide us with our immediate sense experience, but reality and the criteria for what is considered as "real" in the universe is mediated by meaning. Because reality is dynamic and mediated by meaning, what occurs is that reality can constantly change as meaning changes over time.[2] Mystery is the ground of all reality. If we turn to the vastness of the universe to look for meaning and an attempt to make some kind of sense out of what we might call our own reality of life or reality of being, what we more often find is not answers, but silence and not reality, but mystery. On the other hand, it would be difficult for any of us to imagine that our own life would have any meaning unless we thought that the universe has meaning.

Let's face it, most of us desire to lead a meaningful life. We want to be "useful" and "purposeful" and make a difference in the world around us in some small way. At our center, we crave some universal value. But as Christians, we need to recognize that any universal value we have as persons can only be rooted in Christ's love for us in that he loved us first and ultimately gave his life for our redemption. As the incarnate, dynamic, and creative Word (*Logos*) of God, Jesus of Nazareth, following his death on the cross and resurrection, ascended to be the Universal Christ and thus become Lord (*Kyrios*) of the universe and the ultimate intelligibility of universal reality. So, for us as Christians, a better starting point might be the faith we possess, that because of the life, death, and resurrection of Jesus Christ, we might personally find both meaning and reality in the universe, because we believe that the universe has become Christocentric and we are consequently part of the body of Christ and that Christocentric universe.

THE UNIVERSE IS CHRISTOCENTRIC

In its most basic definition, "Christocentrism" indicates that the human personhood assumed by the Son of God in the incarnation is a mystery wrapped in silence, which will bring about the radical renewal of creation, the salvation of humankind, and the ultimate perfection of the universe through the power of love. Though silent and mysterious, we believe that the universe is Christocentric in that Christ was, is, and will be the beginning, the center, and the end goal of all human existence and of the entire universe. The whole universe with Christ as its head is the true end and essence of Christianity, in that all things are now permeated with the special presence of God throughout the universe.[3] The Word spoken into the silence of the universe is Christ, and our own reality is tied up with the same reality as the universality of Christ.

In Pierre Teilhard de Chardin's landmark book *The Phenomenon of Man*,[4] he points out that the universe in terms of the historical process is in dynamic movement from lower to higher. Its movement is from "Unconsciousness to consciousness to self-consciousness and then to Christ-consciousness." Teilhard calls this highest end point, "The Omega Point," which he equates with the Universal or Cosmic Christ.[5] This is the place where the cosmos intersects with God in the Universal Christ, making the entire universe Christocentric. At this intersection, Teilhard envisioned an interplay of what he called the two convergences—the cosmic (natural) and the Christic (supernatural).

Because of "Christ in us," through and with the dynamism of the Holy Spirit, as the power of our self-transcendence (and because the Holy Spirit always points to Christ)—all of our destinies are tied up with the Universal Christ at this meeting point of the universe with Christ. God the Father who created the universe, the resurrected Christ, and the Holy Spirit in us is what makes the universe Christocentric. It brings about ultimate reality and meaning, not only for the whole of the universe, but for us personally as well. In Christ, the universal and the personal are drawn into oneness. The silence of the Christocentric universe can fill our now-moment with meaning, reality, and the intimate presence of Christ if we are not simply waiting for the next moment to come and the next after that.

Furthermore, just because the universe seems silent to us does not necessarily mean that there is nothing going on. In speaking of the silence of the universe, we should not equate silence simply with wordlessness, absence of sound, or even all that we comprehend as silence in a natural sense. Like the supernatural silence of God, the silence of the universe is not to be understood strictly in terms of human silence. The language of God is silence, but in Christ, God has spoken the Word of God into the universe (Jn. 1:1). Thus, the silence of the universe has become infused with the holiness of God.

THE UNIVERSAL CHRIST IN THE NEW TESTAMENT

The Old Testament of the Bible had established a close bond between Yahweh as God and the universe. Beginning in the creation account in the Book of Genesis, this bond then extends throughout many of the Psalms, Wisdom Books, and the Prophets. We find several references to this for example in the Book of the Prophet Jeremiah (Jer. 4:23–36, 5:22–23, 9:9, 10:10, 27:5–6). In the New Testament, the Universal Christ can be described as that aspect of the eternal God in Christ which fills the entire universe and is limitless to time and space. An eternal God would have no bounds or limits.

The intimate link between Christ and the perfection of the universe is justified on New Testament grounds by the victory Christ won through his death on the cross and resurrection as all the forces controlling the universe were made subject to him. In his person, all cohesive power in the universe was centered in Christ. The silence of the universe has been filled with the Logos, i.e., the Word of God. The whole universe had been created out of nothingness, and the Scriptures tell us that the wisdom of God was present at the beginning. Then, the personification of universal wisdom was fully revealed in the pre-existent Christ. Following his resurrection, Jesus Christ received his full role as Lord (Kyrios) of the entire universe.[6]

New Testament references to Jesus of Nazareth becoming the Universal Christ can be found primarily in the Gospel of John as well as in Paul's Letters to the Colossians and the Ephesians:

I. The Preeminence of Christ:

"In the beginning was the Word, and the Word was with God, and the Word was God. He was in the beginning with God. All things came to be through him, and without him nothing came to be. What came to be through him was life, and this life was the light of the human race.

The light shines in the darkness and the darkness has not overcome it"
(Jn. 1: 1–5).

II. The Preeminence of Christ:

"He is the image of the invisible God, the firstborn of all creation. For
in him were created all things in heaven and on earth, the visible and
the invisible, whether thrones or dominions or principalities or pow-
ers; all things were created through him and for him. He is before all
things, and in him all things hold together. He is the head of the body,
the church. He is the beginning, the firstborn from the dead, that in all
things he himself might be preeminent. For in him, all the fullness was
pleased to dwell, and through him to reconcile all things for him, making peace by the blood of his cross [through him], whether those on
earth or those in heaven" (Col. 1:15–20).

III. The Preeminence of Christ:

"He has made known to us the mystery of his will in accord with
his favor that he set forth in him as a plan for the fullness of times, to
sum up all things in Christ, in heaven and on earth. And what is the
surpassing greatness of his power for us who believe, in accord with
the exercise of his great might, which he worked in Christ, raising him
from the dead and seating him at his right hand in the heavens, far above
every principality, authority, power, and dominion, and every name that
is named not only in this age but also in the one to come. And he put
all things beneath his feet and gave him as head over all things to the
church, which is his body, the fullness of the one who fills all things
in every way. And to bring to light [for all] what is the plan of the
mystery hidden from ages past in God who created all things, so that
the manifold wisdom of God might now be made known through the
church to the principalities and authorities in the heavens" (Eph. 1:9–10,
19–23; 3:9–10).[7]

The New Testament verses affirming the Universal Christ were also reaffirmed in the early Christian church through the writings of the Church
Fathers, Ignatius of Antioch, Clement, and Irenaeus. The theology of the
Universal Christ and Christocentrism can also be found in the Middle Ages
in the writings of Thomas Aquinas and Bonaventure, in our current day in
the theologies of Vatican Council II, and more specifically in the theologies
of Jesuits, Teilhard de Chardin and Karl Rahner, as well as the writings of
Franciscan priest and spiritual author, Rev. Richard Rohr.

THE UNIVERSAL CHRIST

Before time began, while silence encompassed the universe, the Infinite Word was in the bosom of the Eternal Father to be spoken into the universe and become incarnate in the fullness of time. And even after the Word was spoken into the silence and made flesh, He would always remain inseparable from the Father and the Holy Spirit. As we continue to discuss the Universal Christ, it should be stated explicitly here that we certainly should not leave behind the Jesus of history. So, I would like to quote the words of that brilliant Jesuit theologian, Teilhard de Chardin whom we briefly mentioned earlier: "The Universal Christ has neither meaning nor value in our eyes except as an expansion of the Christ who was born of Mary and died on the cross."[8]

It is marvelous to consider that the Universal Christ, the Lord of the Cosmos, was once enclosed in the loving womb of his mother and that at one time in history, Jesus' known universe was Mary's womb. The title of "Christ" is not part of Jesus' name. The title confers upon Jesus a universal role that is greater than even Christianity itself as a world religion. Christ is a translation of the Hebrew word, *Masiah—Messiah*, and was a title which came from the Greek word, *Christos*, which means "Anointed One." Following his death, resurrection, and ascension, Jesus of Nazareth would then be considered "the Universal Christ." The early Christian community, in believing that Jesus Christ was the Son of God, also conferred upon him the title *Kyrios* which was the Greek translation for "Lord" or "God." This word appears seven hundred times in the New Testament. Also, the word "catholic" simply means "universal," and when used in religious matters, the term is generally capitalized. "Catholic" was first used by the church Father, Ignatius of Antioch, in 110 A.D.[9]

The Universal Christ can also be seen as the life and love principle of everything in the universe. Therefore, we should make a conscious choice to see God in everyone, in everything, and everywhere. In being universal, Jesus Christ no longer belongs to any particular age, nation, or religion. As stated earlier, one cannot affirm the Universal Christ without affirming Jesus of Nazareth. To do this would make the risen Christ only a cosmic idea or some mythical icon. Jesus of Nazareth is the incarnate human being, fully human; fully divine. Jesus Christ is the eternal cosmic Christ, Lord of the universe. That being said, Jesus of Nazareth, in his life and death on the cross, can be called a person of recorded history as we know it. But there were no actual witnesses to the resurrection as it happened. As regards the resurrection, recorded history is silent. This leaves a question as to whether Jesus' resurrection, when restricted as it is to empty tomb and appearance stories in the Bible, should be viewed as an historical event at all. However, if one believes that the resurrection of Jesus of Nazareth is the Christocentric point in which He became the Universal Christ, then it becomes more than simply an event to be viewed through the lens of recorded history as we know it. Rather, it would make this event something "trans-historical," in that the resurrection of Jesus Christ from the dead would then have a dynamic bearing on both our individual and personal lives as well as the past, present, and future of the entire span of the historical universe.

The New Testament letter to the Hebrews opens with a reflection on the climax of God's revelation to the human race through his Son, Jesus Christ. The divine communication was initiated and maintained during Old Testament times in fragmentary and varied ways through the prophets, including Abraham, Moses, and all persons and prophets through whom God spoke. But now in these last days, the final age, God's revelation of his saving purpose is achieved through one who is God's Son, whose role is redeemer and mediator of all of creation. Jesus Christ has been made heir of all things through his death and resurrection. Yet he existed before he appeared as man, and through him God created the entire universe. The Word became flesh and now Christ is risen. There are no more words, and there is only the silence of God which remains for us to hear in prayer. The Letter to the Hebrews opens with these two verses:

> In times past, God spoke in partial and various ways to our ancestors through the prophets; in these last days, he spoke to us through a Son, whom he made heir of all things and through whom he created the universe. (Heb. 1:1–2)

In attempting to grasp any vision of the Universal Christ, words eventually become useless, and one must spend considerably more time in simple prayerful silence, more time in communion than in conversation. How do we fully comprehend and express that in Christ, we are not only part of the universe, but that the universe is part of us? Or as Paul relates: "In Christ all things hold together and are reconciled" (Col. 1:17, 20).

Finally, part of our personal prayer each morning should be that on this new day we are about to enter, the Lord will be king of our memory, our intellect, our will, our emotions, and our heart. And that our entire being will be completely subject to Him as we invite the Lord to reign in us. So, on this new day, we might proclaim in truth that the Lord is both our King as well as the King and Lord of the entire universe. The Universal Christ must be made personal within us, because by virtue of our Baptism, the Holy Spirit is in us and always points to Christ. We have become part of both the Body of Christ and the evolving Christocentric universe. What is most personal is most universal, and what is most universal is most personal. Therefore, as Christians, our participation in both the Body of Christ and the Christocentric Universe is what gives us our ultimate purpose and meaning in all of reality.

On the other hand, God is love (1 Jn. 4:8, 16); love is expansive and never ends, and reality is dynamic and not static. Therefore, neither we, as loving persons nor the Christocentric universe, are simply static realities of being. Both we and the Christocentric universe are always and continually in the process of evolving and dynamically becoming. For the time being, our full individual meaning and purpose in reality, along with the meaning of the Christocentric universe, must remain as reality wrapped in the mystery of Christ and part of what we have been referring to as "the Holy Silence."

NOTES

1. Rumi, *Twentieth-Century Literature in English*, vol. 3, Manmohan Bhatnagar, ed. (New Delhi: Atlantic Publishing, 1998), p. 15.

2. Michael Hickey, *Get Real* (Lanham, MD: University Press of America, 2012), pp. 3–9.

3. "Christocentric," Merriam Webster, https://www.merriam-webster.com/dictionary/Christocentric.

4. Pierre Teilhard de Chardin, "Phenomenon of Man," Internet Archive, https://archive.org/stream/ThePhenomenonOfMan/phenomenon-of-man-pierre-teilhard-de-chardin_djvu.txt.

5. "Omega Point," Ibid, Ch. 16, f. 4; De Chardin, "Phenomenon of Man."

6. Ibid, Ch. 15, f. 8 (see Sec. 55:1–9, p. 335).

7. Ibid, Ch. 1, f. 3.

8. Pierre Teilhard de Chardin, *The Divine Milieu* (New York: HarperCollins, 1964), p. 117).

9. Ibid, Ch. 15, f. 8 (see Sec. 45:21, 30; 78:70, 87:118. 43:142, 45:21, 50:19, 52:10, 14; 55:10, 23, 29; 79:59–67).

Chapter 17

The Final Word

Christ Himself is the one voice, the one Word, the final Word spoken by God into the universe. It is He who unites all the other words ever heard in the silence of every prayer.

Cover Attribution

Our Lady of Silence

Thanks to the graciousness and kindness of Fr. Emiliano Antenucci, rector of the Sanctuary of Our Lady of Silence Shrine in Avezzano, Italy, I was given permission to use this high-definition copy of their beautiful icon for my new book. The icon which encourages interior silence was blessed by the Holy Father, Pope Francis and signed during a meeting with Fr. Emiliano in 2016. It is on display daily at the sanctuary. The Byzantine style icon depicts Mary, the Mother of God, with a finger to her lips, which is a universal sign of silence. As the Mother of Jesus, Mother of God, Mother of the church universal, and our loving spiritual Mother, there can be no more beautiful and representative icon of Holy Silence.

Index

About the Author

Michael Hickey is a graduate of Northeastern University, Boston, Massachusetts, and a master of divinity studies graduate of Weston Jesuit/ the Boston College School of Theology and Ministry, Boston, Massachusetts.

Following a career as a corporate executive for a Fortune 500 company, he became the director of two 501 C-3 charitable non-profits.

He has had six books previously published: *Get Wisdom, Get Goodness: Virtue Is the Power to Do Good, Get Real: Reality and Mystery, Get to the*

End: A Catholic's View of the End of Times, Catholic Social Teaching and Distributism: Toward a New Economy, and *Themes from the Gospel of John.* The last five books were published by University Press of America and Hamilton Books, divisions of Rowman & Littlefield, Lanham, Maryland.

Hickey is retired and spends the spring and summer with his family in Dartmouth, Massachusetts, and the fall and winter in Naples, Florida. He teaches courses on religion and philosophy at Florida Gulf Coast University, Naples, Florida.

Hickey is married to Theresa, a published poet and the editor of all his books. In their fifty-seven years of marriage, they have raised four happy and "well-adjusted" children into adulthood, and they have seven grandchildren.